The Rediscovery of Ireland's Past:
the Celtic Revival 1830-1930

JEANNE SHEEHY

photographs by GEORGE MOTT

with 177 illustrations, 25 in color

Thames and Hudson

1 *Half-title page:* an ancient Celtic whorl pattern, on the cross of
J. J. Cunningham (d. 1890) in Glasnevin Cemetery, Dublin,
signed 'O'Shea, Kilkenny'. See p. 74.

2 *Title page:* Irish emblems – harps, shamrocks, round towers
and wolfhounds – on the reredos of the Catholic church at
Kilcock, Co. Kildare, 1862, probably by J. J. McCarthy. See p. 72.

Library of Congress Catalog Card Number: 79-63878

Text and monochrome illustrations printed in Great Britain
by Butler & Tanner Ltd, Frome, Somerset
Colour illustrations printed in Great Britain
by Balding & Mansell Ltd, Wisbech, Cambridgeshire
Bound in Great Britain
by Butler & Tanner Ltd, Frome, Somerset

CONTENTS

THE
SPIRIT
OF THE
NATION

CHAPTER 1

Introduction

IRISH CULTURAL LIFE in the nineteenth century was marked by a growing sense of national identity, embracing the whole population, and linked to the Celtic past. It began with a desire for political freedom, already evident in the eighteenth century when there was for a short time a Parliament in Dublin with a fair degree of legislative independence. The Act of Union, which became effective in 1801, dealt a severe blow to Irish freedom, but did not kill it. Opposition to rule from London grew, chiefly voiced by the Protestant middle class. The Catholic Emancipation Act of 1829, which gave civil rights to 'His Majesty's Roman Catholic Subjects', also gave a political identity to the bulk of the population. From then on Ireland was increasingly aware of itself as not only politically but culturally different from England. Leaders of thought began to see the possibility of restoring Ireland's self-respect by drawing attention to her great cultural achievements of the past. This was made possible by the fact that there had been, in Europe generally, a growing interest in history, especially the Middle Ages. In England, for example, such interest resulted chiefly in the Gothic Revival in architecture, though it also came out in painting, and of course in literature.

In Ireland people looked more and more to the past: they looked at the church plate and jewellery which had survived from the Early Christian period, they examined the not inconsiderable architectural remains scattered round the country, and most of all they studied ancient manuscripts for information about Irish history and civilization. They realized that vestiges of this ancient culture remained in the music, storytelling and customs of the Irish-speaking population, and began to study those too. Such interests were already apparent in the late eighteenth century, and they gained momentum in the nineteenth. They began among scholars – historians and antiquarians – who were essentially middle class, but then gradually filtered through to the whole country, so that a people who had been told for years that they were savages, with a barbarous language and no evidence of civilization, were persuaded that this was not so.

The process of rehabilitation was not a rapid one. The benefits of Emancipation were at first felt only by the prosperous Catholic, and in his new-found freedom he was inclined to show that he was as good as any Englishman by imitating that Englishman as closely as possible. The Irish peasant throughout the nineteenth century was still oppressed and abused, and treated with ridicule. The most cruel example of this is the image of the Irishman in *Punch* cartoons and elsewhere, a 22 retarded creature with a low forehead, bulging eyes and a heavy jaw, generally 94 slobbering at the mouth, who comes very low on the evolutionary ladder between apes and Englishmen.[1] Irish people themselves compounded this by behaving as

3 Frontispiece by Frederic Burton for *The Spirit of the Nation*, 1845, a collection of pieces from the newspaper, which was a symbol of nationalism for succeeding generations (see p. 41). Harpists are placed before a Hiberno-Romanesque arch, and the decoration includes Celtic interlace. The shield bottom right bears the Red Hand of Ulster; bottom left, a girl watches the sunrise – often used in imagery (ills. 1, 56), and later emblem of the Fenians.

the propaganda expected them to do. Driven by the miserable condition of their lives, they kept pigs in the kitchen, they fought, and they drank. It is not accidental that one of the pioneers of the crusade against alcohol in the nineteenth century was an Irishman, Father Theobald Mathew. Worst of all, they made fun of themselves, and wrote songs and stories in which they appeared as their enemies saw them. Thus was 'Paddy', the stage Irishman, born; nor has he yet been eradicated.

It has often been suggested, apparently with good reason, that the Irish do not naturally express themselves in art, or possess much aesthetic appreciation of painting, sculpture, architecture and the like. Their natural means of expression, it is maintained, is language, and in this they are highly gifted. It is assumed that this is a basic characteristic; but it could be due more to social and economic factors than to the nature of the Celt. The native Irish possessed great gifts in architecture and applied art in the period from the eighth century until the twelfth, and these survived well into the ensuing period of invasion and conquest. Succeeding centuries of war and hardship gradually wiped them out: the visual arts need leisure, stability, and above all money to flourish and survive. Music, on the other hand, and literature, can be passed on orally even in times of change and instability. Thus the literary talents of the Celt were sustained and developed, used to maintain his cultural identity, even practised as political protest, while his capacity to produce tangible and visible works of art atrophied for lack of use. The result was that by the nineteenth century literary expression came naturally, while artistic expression did not. That he had a latent talent for the visual arts is attested to by the fact that from time to time it erupted, given the chance. The eighteenth century, for example, was one of the great periods for Irish art. It was strongly influenced by England, and was an art of the Protestant Ascendancy, apparently divorced from the bulk of the Irish Catholic population, but for all that it has a character of its own which distinguishes it quite clearly from English art. Many patrons were of the old Celtic stock, or had been settled for so long that they had taken on many of its qualities. A great number of the designers and craftsmen were also Irish. Given the opportunity there was no lack of artistic skill among the native Irish, as witness the quality of the plasterwork, silver, bookbinding, architecture, painting and sculpture they produced in that period.

Had Irish art in the nineteenth century been a matter of continuing the work of the eighteenth, a coherent and distinctly Irish style might have emerged. But the aristocracy, who had been the principal patrons, retired to their country estates, or became absentee landlords, after the first twenty years of the century. Patronage devolved upon the middle classes, whose tastes were different, and the continuity was broken. The change was reinforced by new waves of influence from England and, in the case of applied arts such as plasterwork and metalwork, by techniques of mass-production. The expression of Irish identity became more and more a matter of a return to the language and culture of the early Irish. This was possible in literature, for the Irish language was alive, though only just, and the English spoken by the majority of the population was enriched by it. Art, on the other hand, was cultivated and cherished only by the few. Furthermore, because its last powerful manifestation had been for the Ascendancy, it was mistrusted by those nationalists who believed that the only true Irish were the native inhabitants from before the Norman conquest, or at most those who had been settled in Ireland before the

Reformation, and who were Catholic. Art was not strong enough, in any of its branches, for a common style to emerge which could be recognized as an expression of nationality, on whatever level. If it wished to proclaim its Irishness it was forced back upon recognizably Irish symbols (of which the shamrock is the most obvious example), upon 'Irish' subject-matter, and upon the imitation of models from what was seen as the golden age, the period which produced the Book of Kells, the 'Tara' Brooch and Cormac's Chapel. Preoccupation with these elements was the factor that bound Irish art together in the nineteenth century.

The most obvious way in which nationality could be expressed was by the use of emblems. There were many of these, but the most commonly used were the shamrock, the harp, the Irish wolfhound, and the round tower. The shamrock has become so universal a symbol of Ireland that one might suppose its use to be of great antiquity.[2] In fact it is first mentioned in Tudor times, when it was generally believed in England that the shamrock was a staple part of the Irish diet. Edmund Campion's *Historie of Ireland* (1571) refers to 'shamrotes, water cresses, and other herbs they feed upon'. Spenser's account of the condition of the people of Munster around 1582 describes the famine of the time, adding 'and yf they founde a plotte of water-cresses or shamrokes they flocked as to a feast for the time'. (This may, of course, be explained by the fact that they had nothing else to eat.) And John Derricke's *Image of Ireland* (1581) speaks scathingly of 'their wilde shamrocke manners'.

A hundred years later the shamrock is clearly identified as an Irish symbol. Thomas Dinely, an English gentleman who made a tour of Ireland about 1681, wrote in his *Journal*:

The 17th day of March yeerly is St Patrick's, an immovable feast when ye Irish of all stations and condicions were crosses in their hats, some of pins, some of green ribbon, and the vulgar superstitiously wear shamroges, 3-leaved grass, which they likewise eat (they say) to cause a sweet breath.

He adds that they demand St Patrick's groat of their masters, and go off to the nearest town, and that 'very few of the zealous are found sober at night'. (The idea not only of wearing, but of drowning, the shamrock is evidently not a new one.) It is also interesting that he refers to green ribbon, indicating that the colour had emblematic significance – though officially blue, probably derived from heraldry, was the national colour.[3]

Copper coins, known as St Patrick's halfpennies, produced at Kilkenny some time in the 1660s or 1670s, show the Saint in bishop's robes, holding aloft a three-leaved plant almost as big as his head.[4] The connection between St Patrick and the shamrock (unsupported by any historical evidence) is explained by Caleb Threlkeld in his *Synopsis Stirpium Hibernicarum*, subtitled *A Short Treatise on Native Plants, especially such as grow spontaneously in the vicinity of Dublin*, published in 1727:

This plant is worn by the people in their hats on the 17th day of March yearly, which is called St Patrick's Day, it being a current tradition that, by this three leaved grass, he emblematically set forth to them the mystery of the Holy Trinity. However that be, when they wet their seamar-oge [shamrock], they often commit excess in liquor, which is not a right keeping of a day to the Lord; error generally leading to debauchery.

46

But what in fact *is* the shamrock? A long scholarly controversy surrounds this question. Threlkeld's illustration in 1727 shows *Trifolium pratense album*, the name then current for white clover, now called *Trifolium repens*. The idea that the early writers meant watercress is not convincing, since the shape of the leaf is quite different. But they may have confused shamrock with wood-sorrell, which also has a three-lobed leaf, and of which the Gaelic name, *seamsoge*, has a similar sound. In 1892 the botanist Nathaniel Colgan published a paper in *The Irish Naturalist* in which he gave an account of an attempt to fix the species of the shamrock.[5] Around St Patrick's Day, 17 March, he had sent to him from eleven counties of Ireland thirteen specimens 'each certified by a competent native authority as the true Shamrock, proper to be worn in the hat as the national badge'. He found that he could not name the species reliably on sight, so he planted them, and waited until they flowered. Eight turned out to be *Trifolium minus*, or yellow-flowered clover, the remaining five *Trifolium repens*. The following year he repeated the experiment with shamrock bought in Dublin, or sent from various parts of the country by naturalists, and from Irish-speaking districts by parish priests. Out of thirty-five specimens tested nineteen were *Trifolium repens*, twelve *Trifolium minus*, two *Trifolium pratense*, or purple clover, and two *Medicago lupulina*, or black medick. The reason for this variety is that in March, in the early stages of their development, it is difficult to tell the species of clover apart, and black medick at the same period is virtually indistinguishable from clover. It is certain that in Ireland clover and shamrock are regarded as quite distinct. There is an Irish name, *seamar*, for clover, and besides it does not have the characteristics attributed to shamrock: this is said never to flower, and to refuse to grow on alien soil. The conclusion must be that shamrock has no objective existence.

5 Lord Charlemont, a tuft of shamrock in his hat, sits in the middle of a group of gentleman-musicians, sketched by Sir Joshua Reynolds for his caricature 'School of Athens', 1751.

In art the shamrock begins to make a regular appearance in the eighteenth century. A caricature by Sir Joshua Reynolds dating from 1751 shows four gentlemen with musical instruments, each with an emblem in his hat – one a leek, another (the Irish peer Lord Charlemont) a large bunch of shamrock. By the early nineteenth century its use had become widespread. In the National Museum of Ireland in Dublin there is an engraved glass goblet commemorating the visit to Dublin in 1821 of George IV. It is decorated with wreaths of shamrocks, and the inscription *Caed Mille Failte* ('a hundred thousand welcomes', misspelt). When the Theatre Royal in Dublin was opened in the same year, it had Neo-Greek decoration on the first circle, while the second circle had a 'Greek chain' twined with the shamrock.[6] Medals too, in the early nineteenth century, frequently show shamrocks. As early as 1801 a medal to celebrate the Union has oaks entwined with shamrocks, the most usual device commemorative of that event, the oak in this case being the symbol of England. It occasionally appears also as a symbol of Ireland, because of the renown of Irish oakwoods. The traditional weapon of the fighting Irishman was the shillelagh – a cudgel of oak, named after the village of Shillelagh, in Co. Wicklow, famous for its oak. Crosby's *Irish Musical Repository*, published about 1810, has a song about an Irishman with the refrain 'With his sprig of shillelah and shamrock so green'.

The second most commonly found Irish emblem is the harp.[7] It is said to have appeared on the Irish Arms in the reign of Henry VIII, and was certainly quartered in the Royal Arms of Britain in the reign of James I. Of its adoption the Earl of Northampton, the Deputy Earl Marshal, is said to have observed that he 'had no affection for the change; that for the adoption of the harp the best reason he could assign was that it resembled Ireland in being such an instrument that it required more cost to keep it in tune than it was worth'. In the eighteenth century the harp frequently found as an Irish emblem has a female figure forming one side. In the nineteenth the favourite model was the so-called Harp of Brian Boru, now in Trinity College, Dublin. As a brooch design it was made popular by Dublin jewellers from the 1850s onwards. Its familiarity today is due to two causes: in 1862 it was adopted as a trademark by Guinness's Brewery,[8] and in 1926 it was incorporated into the new Irish Free State coinage. It is also used as a symbol of the Irish Government, for example on uniforms and printed documents.

6 The 'Harp of Brian Boru', made some time between the 13th and 16th centuries. The historic Brian Boroimhe was killed in 1014.

The Irish wolfhound, in its present form, may be said to be a product of the Celtic revival.[9] It was originally a very large hound used for hunting wolves and deer, peculiar to Ireland but valued throughout Europe. There are frequent references to wolfhounds in the ancient stories of Fionn and Oisín – Fionn had a favourite hound called Bran, and another called Sceolaing. In the fourth century there is a reference to seven Irish dogs being sent to Rome for 'solemn shows and games', and they were much prized in later times. The early seventeenth-century Spanish poet Lope de Vega wrote a sonnet on one. By the early nineteenth century, however, they had nearly died out: some say they were extinct by the 1830s or 1840s. Yet when the Irish Wolfhound Club was founded in 1885 Captain Graham, an authority on the breed, compiled the pedigrees of about 300 dogs. Many of these had been bred from whatever vestiges of the old breed remained, crossed with Scottish deerhounds. They seem to have been selected by comparison with descriptions of Irish wolfhounds, of which there were numerous accounts and even images. There was certainly great interest in the hound in the nineteenth century, and it often appeared as an emblem, either accompanying a figure of Hibernia or Erin or in a group with a round tower and shamrock.

56
61
1

The round tower was the fourth popular symbol, chosen because it was peculiar to Ireland (with a few examples in the west of Scotland), and also probably because of its mystery. It was only in the mid-nineteenth century that the Christian origin of round towers was established (see below, pp. 20–22): before that they were the object of speculation as varied as it was eccentric.

Another manner by which an Irish character was conveyed was the use, in painting and sculpture, of Irish subject-matter. This can be traced back to the eighteenth century. The decoration designed for the Four Courts in Dublin by James Gandon (1743–1823) included medallions representing figures connected, in antiquity, with the law, and among them was Ollamh Fodhla, who was supposed to have given the ancient laws to the Irish. The Neo-Classical artist James Barry (1741–1806) exhibited a painting entitled *St Patrick baptizing the King of Cashel* (now destroyed) before the Dublin Society in 1763. The decoration of St Patrick's Hall in Dublin Castle, executed by Vincent Waldré (d. 1814) about 1795, includes two Irish subjects, *St Patrick lighting the Pascal Fire on the Hill of Slane* and *Henry II meeting the Irish Leaders.* The decoration was not completed until much later, possibly for the visit of George IV in 1821, and it is interesting that in the finished version of *Henry II* there is a round tower in the background which does not appear in Waldré's sketch. All the foregoing instances of Irish subject-matter, except for the painting by Barry, can be explained by reference to the buildings they were to decorate.[10] In addition, their evocations of Ireland's remote history suited the romantic tastes of the time. In the 1840s subjects from Irish history or everyday life became a common way of expressing nationality.

7

The third, and ultimately the most powerful, expression of Irishness was by the imitation of ancient models. This did not get properly under way until the middle of the nineteenth century, but it, too, can be seen to have its roots in the eighteenth century, when interest began to be aroused in the literary remains of ancient Ireland, and in her antiquities. The great Charles O'Conor of Belnagare collected and studied ancient Irish manuscripts, and published *Dissertations on the Ancient History of Ireland* in 1753. He was, oddly enough, encouraged in his work by Dr Johnson, who urged

7 Vincent Waldré: *Henry II meeting the Irish Leaders*, a ceiling painting in Dublin Castle, designed *c.* 1795 and executed, with the addition of a round tower in the left background, *c.* 1821.

him to 'give a history of the Irish nation from the conversion to Christianity to the invasion from England'. Interest in ancient history and legend was also stimulated by MacPherson's *Ossian*, which first appeared in 1762. It purported to be a translation of the poems of the Celtic hero Ossian, though in fact it seems to have been composed by MacPherson on a basis of Highland folklore. Ancient Irish poems did exist, mostly written down in the early Middle Ages but drawn from earlier sources, which dealt with Celtic heroes who were Irish, not Scottish, and bore similar names – Fionn, whom MacPherson called Fingal, and Oisín, whom Mac-Pherson called Ossian. The fact that MacPherson caught the imagination of Romantic Europe was an added reason for looking at the Irish sources. Interest in

ancient Irish culture was consolidated in the nineteenth century, when a great number of societies were founded for the study of Ireland's past. The earliest of these was the Gaelic Society of Dublin, which held its first meeting in January 1807, and announced in the initial volume of its *Transactions* (1808):

> The Society recommends itself to every liberal, patriotic, and enlightened Mind; an opportunity is now, at length, offered to the Learned of Ireland, to retrieve their Character among the Nations of Europe, and shew that their History and Antiquities are not fitted to be consigned to eternal oblivion.

This statement, with its suggestion of national pride, and rebuilding of Irish self-esteem, set the tone for the rest of the century.

CHAPTER 2

The antiquarians

ALTHOUGH SCHOLARS, ANTIQUARIANS and topographical artists of the eighteenth century had shown an interest in Irish antiquities from time to time, the first really fruitful and concerted study of them came in the early nineteenth century. The years from 1830 to the Great Famine of the later 1840s were a period of great cultural and political activity, one of the peaks of Irish life in the nineteenth century. The achievements of these years remain as monuments in their own right, but they also formed a basis on which later generations could build.

One of the most important figures of the period, as an antiquarian, a topographical artist, a journalist, a musician, and the centre of a lively group of like-minded and talented men, was George Petrie (1790–1886).[1] As early as 1808, when he was 13 eighteen, he made a tour in Co. Wicklow and commented extensively on its antiquities and on its music. He trained as an artist, so that the coming into fashion, about 1820, of illustrated guidebooks allowed him to earn his living as a topographical artist, to such an extent that hardly an illustrated book appeared in Ireland in the first half of the nineteenth century without some contribution by Petrie. Since many of the most picturesque sites had architectural remains his work as an artist was enriched by, and reinforced, his antiquarian studies.

In 1828 he became a member of the Royal Irish Academy, and was elected to its council in 1829. The Academy, which had been founded in the eighteenth century for the advancement of learning, was in a depressed state, particularly as regards antiquarian studies. Petrie began to organize its museum, gathering together the bits and pieces which were already in its possession, but scattered about, and adding new ones. Among its most spectacular acquisitions were the Cross of Cong and some torcs from Tara, acquired in 1839, the 'Tara' Brooch found in 1850 and 9 acquired by the Academy in 1868, and the Ardagh Chalice, bought also in 1868. 10 Because of the collection, and also because of the scholars it drew together, the Academy became an important centre for the development of interest in Ireland's national heritage. The museum was among the leading attractions for visitors to Dublin. Even Thomas Carlyle, in his acid and unsympathetic notes on a tour in Ireland in 1849, was obliged to praise it as 'really an interesting Museum, for everything has a certain authenticity, as well as national and other significance, too often wanting in such places'.[2]

8 Antiquarians or tourists inspecting the high cross of Monasterboice, from O'Neill's *The Most Interesting of the Sculptured High Crosses of Ancient Ireland*, 1857. See p. 23.

Petrie's forays into journalism were also important – first in the *Dublin Penny Journal*, launched on 30 June 1832 by Caesar Otway (1780–1842), and later in his 4 own *Irish Penny Journal*, whose short life began in 1840. Their aim was to draw the attention of Irish people to the subjects most likely to interest them, next to politics and polemics: 'the history, biography, poetry, antiquities, natural history,

legends and traditions of the country'.[3] In this they were ahead of the Young Ireland newspaper *The Nation*, though the latter reached a much wider audience, and had 21 much greater popular appeal. All three publications had in common their anxiety to steer clear of sectarianism.

The business of religion is an important one in nineteenth-century Ireland, and more complex than it at first appears. Although attitudes had not hardened as they were to do later in the century, there was a good deal of bigotry about, and bitterness between Catholics and Protestants was, in some people, very strong. Catholics saw themselves as the heirs of Ireland's past, and Protestants as foreign usurpers. Protestants, the descendants of successive waves of settlers, regarded themselves, justifiably, as Irish: they were certainly not English. It was from the Protestant middle class (the nobility and landed gentry were, on the whole, indifferent) that the drive for an Irish national identity mostly came. But the vision that they saw was not of a free, *Catholic*, Ireland. The more liberal among them envisaged a country in which people of different religions were equal. Other Protestants feared that Irish freedom would mean Catholic ascendancy and therefore Rule from Rome. Daniel O'Connell (1775–1847), by pushing Catholic Emancipation through Parliament, freed Irish Catholics – the middle classes at any rate – from their social, political and professional disabilities. He then turned his attention to the repeal of the Act of Union, using the vast Catholic power he had unleashed, thereby associating the idea of Irish nationalism with Roman Catholicism. Caesar Otway is an interesting illustration of one Protestant attitude of the period. He founded the *Dublin Penny Journal*, with its aim of fostering a national identity, and was described by a contemporary as a 'distinguished and patriotic clergyman'. Yet he was quite bigoted in

9, 10 The most famous of all Irish antiquities, discovered in 1850 and 1868. *Opposite*, the 'Tara' Brooch, made *c.* 700 of bronze overlaid with gold, amber and glass (about twice actual size). *Below*, the contemporary Ardagh Chalice, of silver enriched with gold filigree and enamels (slightly more than half actual size). Their forms and ornamentation were much imitated in Celtic Revival metalwork (see ills. 11, 70, 76, 124, 125).

his comments on the building of Catholic churches in the years after Emancipation. Tuam Cathedral, for example, had 'a pretending, assuming, *falsetto* look – a Brummagem imitation!!' and was 'a monument of the ambition, shall I say the taste of the Connaught hierarchy'.[4] Petrie himself, who, it can be argued, did as much in the long run for Ireland's self-respect as Daniel O'Connell, was Protestant, and of a family only recently settled in Ireland. On the other hand two of his friends and colleagues, leading scholars of the revival and contributors to Otway's *Dublin Penny Journal*, Eugene O'Curry (1796–1862) and John O'Donovan (1809–61), were Catholic.

Another important enterprise in which Petrie was a major figure was the historical department of the Ordnance Survey of Ireland. The Survey entailed the collection of a great deal of information on the geology and natural history of the country. In addition, in order to fix on the correct spelling of place names antiquarian research was done on topography and history, both on the spot and from manuscripts. This work was carried out by the historical department under Petrie, whose principal assistants were O'Curry and O'Donovan. The information collected was to be published, as essential to the elucidation of the maps, in an accompanying memoir. A sample, the *Memoir of the Parish of Templemore*, was presented to the British Association in 1835 and published in 1837. Then the Government decided to stop publication of further memoirs, and to disband the historical department. It did this in spite of the recommendations of a Parliamentary Commission and protests from leading learned bodies such as the British Association and the Royal Irish Academy. The reasons given were financial, but there have also been suggestions that the Government felt that the Survey was generating too much interest in Irish antiquities, and thus feeding national sentiment.[5] Certainly, by providing regular salaries for Petrie, O'Donovan and O'Curry, it permitted antiquarian research on a scale which might not otherwise have been possible, and this was an important ingredient in the strong national awareness of the 1840s and 1850s.

Petrie was the founder of systematic and scientific archaeology in Ireland. With O'Curry and O'Donovan he was revolutionary in putting together evidence from ancient manuscripts and from investigations on the sites themselves. His work countered two tendencies among historians of Ireland. On the one hand there were those who claimed that the native Irish were savages, and had always been so: they included men like Bishop Brinkley of Cloyne, 'who could only discern, in the long vista of Ireland's past history, some faint shadowings of naked unskilled savages, lurking in the obscurity of primeval forests, or basking in their lairs, ignorant of every art'.[6] On the other hand there were those who developed glamorous accounts of ancient Ireland from the more colourful flights of the Irish bards.

Petrie's work on the Irish round towers was of particular importance. This was presented as a paper to the Royal Irish Academy in 1833, and published in his book *On the Ecclesiastical Architecture of Ireland* in 1845. The towers had been the subject of speculation for some time, and a great deal of controversy surrounded them; indeed it was said that a ready method of testing the sanity of an Irish antiquary was to ask his opinion as to the origin of the round towers. Petrie analysed and considered the various theories, a task which required, according to his biographer William Stokes, 'the constant exercise of a calm and philosophic spirit'. Particularly irritating were the writers who tried to establish the original use of the towers

11, 12 George Petrie's *Pilgrims at Clonmacnoise*, a watercolour of *c.* 1838 (National Gallery of Ireland), and a view of the site, showing how Petrie rearranged the buildings to include more interesting details, and dramatized the fall of the land.

13 George Petrie in old age: a miniature by Bernard Mulrenin (National Gallery of Ireland).

through etymology, 'of some of whom it may be said, that they possessed no accurate knowledge of any language, even of their own'.[7] These arrived at the conclusion that the towers were temples for the holy fire of the Arch Druids, of Phoenician construction, or built by the African sea-champions; sorcerer's towers; pillars for celestial observation; towers for dancing round after the manner of the Canaanites in honour of the heavens; towers for the proclamation of anniversaries; towers for the Persian or Chaldean Magi; temples of Vesta; astronomical gnomons; phallic temples; Danish watch-towers; sepulchral monuments. Petrie looked at the various theories, and disposed of them. He established that the towers were of Christian origin, could not have been built before the introduction of Christianity into Ireland, and were designed as belfries, and as strongholds for people and precious objects in case of attack.[8]

Tangible evidence of Petrie's work also survives in his painting – for in spite of his reputation in other fields it was as a topographical artist that he earned his living, except for the years he spent in the Ordnance Survey. His father was a miniature painter, and the companions of his youth were painters. In 1813 he set out with James Arthur O'Connor (1792–1841) and Francis Danby (1793–1861) on a trip to London, where they looked at art collections and met Benjamin West. He contributed to numerous guidebooks and collections of views. Like so many artists of the period in Ireland he worked mainly in watercolours. One of his best known pictures is *The Last Round of the Pilgrims at Clonmacnoise*. This was first painted in 11 1828, for the album of Mrs Haldiman. Many years later, about 1838 or 1839, after the break up of the Ordnance Survey historical department, he repeated the subject for the Royal Irish Art Union, and wrote a long letter to them explaining it:[9]

> I trust also that it will be apparent that my aim was something beyond that of the ordinary class of portrait landscape, and, therefore, more difficult of attainment. It was my wish to produce an Irish picture somewhat historical in its object, and poetical in its sentiment – a landscape composed of several of the monuments characteristic of the past history of our country, and which will soon cease to exist, and to connect with them the expression of human feelings equally belonging to our history, and which are destined to a similar extinction.
>
> In short, I desired to produce a picture which might have an interest and value, not merely pictorial, beyond the present time, and thus connect my name with that of the Art Union Association, and with the history of art in Ireland. And, with this feeling, I did my best to adhere to local as well as general truth at whatever cost to the pictorial attraction of the work, and to adopt such a treatment of effect as might conduce to the sentiment of the picture without unfitting it for the purpose of a popular print, if it should ever be deemed worthy to be engraved.

Though he had visited Clonmacnoise in 1818, and made over three hundred draw- 12 ings of the monuments there, he did not in fact adhere so very closely to 'local truth'. Individual details and objects are accurate, but he has altered their grouping, and the fall of the ground, to obtain a more picturesque and dramatic effect.

In one of the collections of Irish views, *Picturesque Sketches of some of the Finest Landscapes and Coast Scenery of Ireland* (1835), Petrie collaborated with two other interesting topographical artists, Andrew Nicholl and Henry O'Neill. Nicholl (1804–86) is most admired for his landscapes with flowers, and for his exotic views in Ceylon (he was for a time master of Drawing and Painting at the Colombo Academy), but he also drew and painted Irish antiquities. Albums of his work done

14 Frederic Burton: *Paddy Coneely, the blind piper* – a watercolour of the musician from whom Petrie collected 17 tunes in 1839 (National Gallery of Ireland). Petrie wrote about Coneely in the *Irish Penny Journal* for 3 October 1840.

in the 1830s and 1840s (several of them in the Ulster Museum, Belfast) are full of views of places like Glendalough, Monasterboice, Muckross and Clonmacnoise, with notes which indicate that he studied the subject, and was familiar with the writings of Petrie and O'Curry.

Henry O'Neill (1798–1880)[10] is best known for his book *The Most Interesting of the Sculptured High Crosses of Ancient Ireland*, published in 1857. It is very accurate in an antiquarian sense, with faithful representations of the crosses, and the ornament upon them, and shows both details and groups of monuments. As with Petrie's *Pilgrims at Clonmacnoise*, the treatment is highly romantic, however, with dramatic groupings and changes of scale. O'Neill was involved in the political movements of his time, and was a member of Daniel O'Connell's Repeal Association. He painted O'Connell and his fellow prisoners in Richmond Jail in 1843, and in 1868 wrote a pamphlet attacking landlordism, entitled *Ireland for the Irish*. His lithographed portrait of an Irish traditional musician, *Gandsey, the Kerry Minstrel*, was offered a prize in the Royal Irish Art Union of 1842. Like Petrie, he wrote on antiquarian subjects; and in fact he tried to refute Petrie and establish the pagan origin of the round towers.

An artist with an interest in Irish antiquities, and also in contemporary life in Gaelic Ireland, was Frederic Burton (1816–1900), who was infinitely more talented as a painter than either Petrie or O'Neill.[11] He was a friend and travelling companion of Petrie: they explored the coast of Kerry together in 1841, and later Burton sent Petrie sketches of beehive dwellings near Dingle. It was also, presumably, on one of Petrie's music collecting trips that Burton painted the Galway piper Paddy Coneely; a print after the watercolour was published in the *Irish Penny Journal* for 3 October 1840.

Another member of the circle of leading antiquarians was Samuel Ferguson (1810–86), a lawyer by profession, born in Belfast.[12] When quite young he became interested in Irish antiquities, and met O'Donovan, O'Curry, and Petrie, with whom he corresponded and to whom he sent sketches and copies of inscriptions from ancient monuments. He learnt Irish, and was interested in Irish music. In later years he was, politically, a Unionist, that is he was in favour of Ireland's legislative union with England, but in his youth he sympathized with the poets and patriots of Young Ireland 'while their aims were directed to a restoration of Grattan's Parliament', and was fond of Thomas Davis (see p. 29), for whom he wrote a most moving lament. Apart from his antiquarian studies, Ferguson's main contribution to the Irish revival was in his poetry, which drew largely on early Irish history and legends. One of his poems, *The Cromlech on Howth*, was published in 1861 in an edition which is a very interesting example of the revival of Celtic ornament. It has a lavish green and gold cover, with interlace patterns, and is embellished inside with decorations from the books of Kells and of Durrow, vividly coloured in scarlet and green, yellow and purple. Though the use of Celtic interlace ornament became very common on book covers later in the century, this is an unusually early example. The illuminations were designed by Margaret Stokes, and were much admired by Burton, who found them 'exquisite'. The book includes notes revised by Petrie on Celtic ornamental art. 17 15

Margaret Stokes (1832–1900) was the daughter of William Stokes (1804–78), a very distinguished Dublin physician.[13] As a doctor he attended Thomas Davis (who died at the age of thirty-one when apparently recovering from cholera), and James Clarence Mangan, in their last illnesses. Mangan (1803–49), a poet and member of the Young Ireland group, was admitted in a dying state to the Meath Hospital when Stokes was making his rounds. Stokes saw that he was properly taken care of and, when he died, was so struck by the beauty of his face that he sent for Burton to make a drawing. Stokes was not an artist, but had become interested in art through his sisters, who were taught by Petrie and by James Arthur O'Connor. He, too, was an amateur of Irish antiquities. Burton and Petrie were his 'favourite artists and dearest friends' and he wrote a solid, comprehensive and sympathetic biography of the latter. Two of his children made important contributions to Irish studies, Margaret as an antiquarian, Whitley (1830–1909) as a philologist. 148

Another Dublin doctor who was also an antiquarian was Stokes's friend and pupil Sir William Wilde (1815–76). He is perhaps best remembered as the parent of Oscar, whose very names are an indication of the antiquarian interests of his father and the romantic nationalism of his mother:[14] the sons of Dublin doctors of the mid-nineteenth century were much more likely to be called William or Henry or George than Oscar Fingal O'Flahertie. Wilde was elected to the Royal Irish Academy in 1839, and made a catalogue of its collection of antiquities. His wife, Jane Francesca Elgee, wrote in the Young Ireland newspaper *The Nation* under the pseudonym Speranza. Their son Oscar was not well known in later life as a Hibernophile, but in his youth he seems to have shared some of his parents' interests, and in 1877 he published an article in *Saunders News-Letter* on 'the unfortunate author of "Irish Crosses"', Henry O'Neill.

So many people were interested in the study of Irish antiquities that they naturally formed themselves into societies, though most also belonged to the Royal Irish

15 Margaret Stokes: titlepage of Samuel Ferguson's *The Cromlech on Howth*, 1861. The capital T in the form of a dragon comes directly from the Book of Kells.

The Cromlech on Howth

·S·Ferguson·

·mdccclxi·

Academy. A group called the Irish Archaeological Society held its inaugural meeting in 1841. Petrie was on its council, and O'Donovan and O'Curry were among the first to work for it. One of its earliest resolutions is interesting for the revival of Irish art: it decided to have an ornamental initial letter engraved for each Irish work or tract that it printed, to be taken from 'some remarkable Irish manuscript'.[15] It was felt that this would be a good way of collecting specimens of ancient Irish calligraphy and would also, perhaps,

> assist in removing the prejudice, or scepticism, that has unreasonably prevailed on the subject of the ancient literature of Ireland; a prejudice which is founded chiefly, if not entirely, upon ignorance, and which cannot better be assailed than by laying before the learned public specimens of what Irish artists of the middle ages really did effect; since it must be evident, that a people, whose literary remains are adorned with such exquisite designs of penmanship could hardly have been the rude and ignorant barbarians that it has hitherto been the fashion to represent them.

Unfortunately, the scheme seems to have come to nothing.

The Celtic Society was founded in 1845, but merged with the Irish Archaeological Society in 1853. Apart from the study and translation of ancient manuscripts it also aimed at protecting 'the existing monumental and architectural remains of Ireland, by directing public attention to their preservation from the destruction with which they frequently are threatened'.[16] Another association, the Kilkenny Archaeological Society, was founded in 1849.

Dublin in the mid-nineteenth century being not so very unlike Dublin now, all of these people whom we have been considering met frequently, on public occasions and in each other's houses. Thomas Carlyle on his tour in 1849 had a letter of introduction to Dr Stokes, and met several of them at dinner in his house in Merrion Square. He is worth quoting, since his descriptions, though unflattering, are more vivid and personal than other accounts.[17] Stokes himself he found a 'clever, energetic, but squinting, rather fierce, sinister-looking man'; Petrie 'a Painter of Landscapes, notable antiquarian, enthusiastic for Brian Boru and all that province of affairs; an excellent simple, affectionate lovable soul ... called for punch instead of wine, he, and was gradually imitated; a thin, wrinkly half ridiculous, yet mildly dignified man; old bachelor, you could see'. (In fact Petrie was married, had several children, and was an enthusiastic family man.) Burton appears as 'a young Portrait-Painter, thin-aquiline man, with long thin locks scattered about, with a look of real painter-talent, but thin, proud-vain; not a pleasant "man of genius"'. Carlyle does not seem to have been any more popular with his hosts than they were with him.

Another, more brilliant, social occasion was the meeting in Dublin in 1857 of the British Association. After the meeting the Ethnological Section, seventy in number, embarked on a trip to the Aran Islands organized by Sir William Wilde.[18] The ship, with its 'freight of Ethnologists and Antiquaries', sailed from Galway to Inishmore, where the antiquities of the island were examined. The highlight of the visit was a feast on the 'velvet turf' of the ancient fort of Dun Aengus. The Provost of Trinity presided, and the meeting was addressed by Wilde. The proceedings attracted the attention of the local people, who gathered around, looking picturesque, 'The men in white woollen fabrics and with sandalled feet, the women and children attired in red of various tints.' O'Donovan and O'Curry addressed them in Irish, 'exhorting them to preserve the old monuments, so many of which had become dilapidated since the time of Petrie's first visit' (in 1822). When the meeting was over Petrie and his friends stayed behind for a fortnight. They took a cottage in the village of Kilronan, Ferguson sent for his wife, and Stokes for his daughter Margaret. To the cottage, in the evenings, musicians would come, and crowds of local people, 'the rich colours of whose dress, heightened by the firelight, showed with a strange vividness and variety' – a convivial version of the scene captured by Burton in *The Aran Fisherman's Drowned Child*. Petrie, with his manu- 25 script music book and his violin, learnt the tunes, and O'Curry took down the words. The party hired a Galway hooker or turf boat, and, taking the 'local anti-quary' on board, sailed from island to island. They also took on board as many local singers as they could hear of, and once again Petrie learnt the tunes and played them on his violin while O'Curry wrote down the words in Irish. They were trans-lated into English by Whitley Stokes. Painting and drawing were not neglected either: Burton painted the islanders, and he, Margaret Stokes and Samuel Ferguson sketched the ruins and other antiquarian objects.

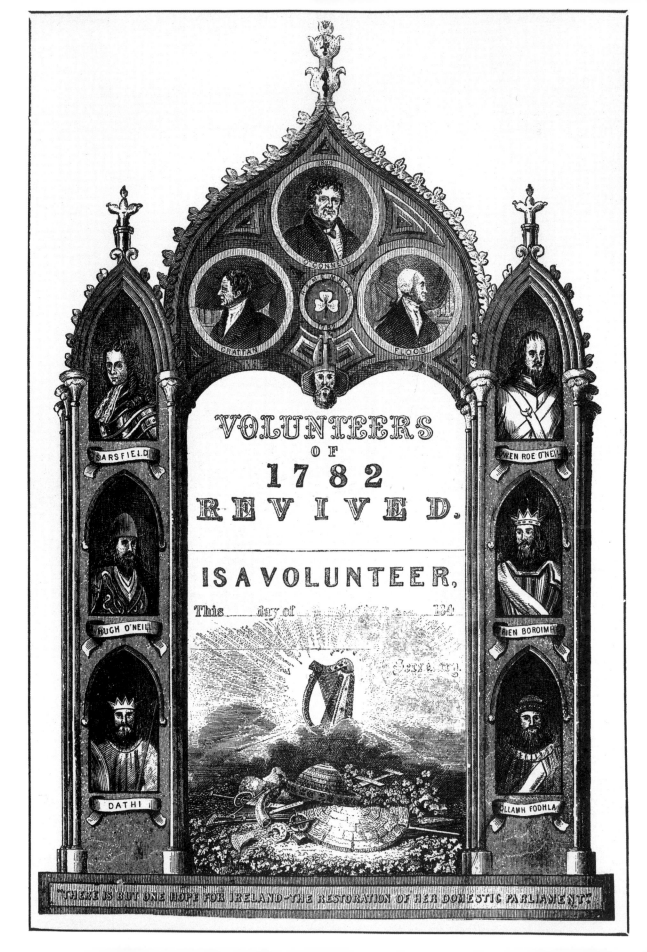

VOLUNTEERS
OF
1782
REVIVED.

IS A VOLUNTEER,

This   day of   184

O'CONNELL

GRATTAN

FLOOD

SARSFIELD

WEN ROE O'NEIL

HUGH O'NEILL

BRIEN BOROIMH

DATHI

OLLAMH FODHLA

"THERE IS BUT ONE HOPE FOR IRELAND—THE RESTORATION OF HER DOMESTIC PARLIAMENT."

CHAPTER 3

Young Ireland

THERE SEEMS TO HAVE BEEN, in nineteenth-century Ireland, a growing sense of the connection between culture and an awareness of nationality. In the case of the antiquarians the initial impulse came from the pursuit of learning, which in turn generated a knowledge of, and respect for, the cultural achievements of Ireland in the Early Christian period. In a limited circle of scholars and antiquarians at first, gradually reaching a wider public, pride in the period before the Norman invasions, and in the vestiges of that civilization which still remained, was awakened. It was a younger generation than the antiquarians, the idealistic young men of the Young Ireland movement, who set out to exploit, for political ends, both Irish antiquities and contemporary Irish art.

After the achievement of Catholic Emancipation in 1829, Daniel O'Connell concentrated on the repeal of the Act of Union. In 1840 he founded the Repeal Association, within which, in the next few years, a group of young men rose to prominence, mostly law students or recently-qualified barristers dedicated to raising the national consciousness of Ireland, and to obtaining political freedom. They gradually drew apart from O'Connell ('Old Ireland'), especially as some of their number came to favour the use of force to obtain the second aim. The most important adherent of Young Ireland was Thomas Osborne Davis (1814–45). He was educated at Trinity College, Dublin, and in 1837 published a pamphlet on the reform of the House of Lords, proposing an elected upper house. In 1838 he was called to the bar, and in 1842, together with Charles Gavan Duffy (1816–1903) and John Blake Dillon, he founded a newspaper called *The Nation*, which was the voice of the movement. The motto it adopted was 'To create and foster public opinion in Ireland, and to make it racy of the soil'.[1] It aimed to develop a sense of national identity which would draw together the various sections of Irish society, emphasizing a common cultural heritage. 'On the neutral ground of ancient history and native art, Unionists and Nationalists could meet without alarm.'[2] It was deliberately non-sectarian. The Young Irelanders themselves came from varied religious backgrounds: Davis was a Protestant, son of a surgeon in the Royal Artillery, and only partly Irish, Dillon was a Catholic from Co. Mayo, and Gavan Duffy a Catholic from Monaghan, an Ulster county. In a sense these men ran counter to O'Connell, who, in order to harness the full power of the Irish people, identified Irish nationalism with Catholicism. Neither O'Connell nor Young Ireland, for all their nationalist fervour, wished for separation from the British Crown: what they desired was simply independence from Westminster.

The first issue of *The Nation*, which appeared on 15 October 1842, had articles by Davis, Gavan Duffy and Dillon, and poetry by Mangan and John Cornelius

16 Membership card of the Repeal Association, with Irish symbols in the centre and heroes round the edge. Notice the Irish crown on Ollamh Fodhla (bottom right) and in the trophy group. See p. 37.

O'Callaghan. The paper also published articles by Petrie, O'Donovan and O'Curry. Gavan Duffy later claimed that they were 'delighted to see studies which they had pursued in the shade and without sympathy become popular':[3] this is an exaggeration, for they were all, Petrie in particular, established and respected. What the paper did for them was to open a wider popular audience than had been available to them through the publications of learned societies and the *Dublin* and *Irish Penny Journals*. It was widely read throughout the country, by groups of people in the smithy or pub, or after Mass on Sundays. 'Dined, and sat down to read *The Nation* at the drawing-room fire, with my glass of punch beside me', wrote Petrie to Lord Adare in 1845.[4] *The Nation* fostered an interest in Irish antiquities through its articles, and exhorted people to 'watch over our historical places, they are in the care of the people, and they are ill cared [for] ... but these ruins were rich possessions'.[5]

Davis in particular was interested in the fine arts, and had strong convictions about their place in the raising of national consciousness. Of the Art Union competition for works illustrating Irish history he wrote:[6]

> We entreat our artists as they love their country, as they owe it a service, as they pity its woes and errors, as they are wroth at its sufferings, and as they hope to share and aid its advance, to use this opportunity of raising the taste and cultivating the nationality of Ireland.

In his fervent desire to create and foster a national art Davis tried to enlist the help of Frederic Burton, who, though politically opposed to Young Ireland ideals (he was a Unionist), was a close friend of his. It was one of Davis's gifts that he could inspire deep affection even in political opponents like Burton or Samuel Ferguson. Burton was not very hopeful of a national art: free, spiritual, high-aiming art, he said, could not be forced.[7] Certain hundreds of pounds would never produce either art or nationality; other phases would only follow if Ireland had a decided national school of poetry. This was a sound observation: painting in Ireland has tended to lag behind literature.

Nevertheless, Davis persevered. He felt that art was essential to the national renown of Ireland, and that the best step towards achieving it was to collect and make known the works of her best artists, living and dead. To create a mass of great pictures, statues, and buildings, he said, ennobled a people in the same way as to create great poems or histories, or make great codes or win great battles. He published in *The Nation* a list of suggestions for historical subjects in painting, which, he said, had been loosely jotted down by a friend.[8] Because he was writing in the mid-nineteenth century the idea of national art was bound up for him with subject-matter, not with style:[9]

> When we speak of high art, we mean art used to instruct and ennoble men; to teach them great deeds, whether historical, religious, or romantic; to awaken their piety, their pride, their justice, and their valour; to paint the hero, the martyr, the rescuer, the lover, the patriot, the friend, the saint, and the Saviour.

The subjects he suggested number about eighty, and are taken from sources like Keating's history (1629), or the *Histoire de l'Irlande* (1758–63) by the Abbé James McGeoghegan, from memoirs, from the *Tracts* of the Archaeological Society, and from that great source of nineteenth-century patriotic sentiment, the ballads of Tom Moore (1779–1852). They range from remote history (*The Landing of the Milesians*

17 Frederic Burton:
Thomas Davis, sketched
as a memorial after
Davis's early death in
1845 (National Gallery
of Ireland).

(see p. 38), *Ollamh Fodhla Presenting his Laws to his People*) through the arrival of
St Patrick (*St Patrick brought before the Druids at Tara*), the Norman invasion (*O'Brien,
O'Connor and McCarthy making Peace to Attack the Normans*) and the struggles of
the ensuing centuries, to modern subjects like *The Clare Election, O'Connell's Dublin* 19
Corporation Speech, and *Father Mathew administering the Pledge in a Munster County*.
His last subject sounds very revolutionary indeed, *The Lifting of the Irish Flags of
a National Fleet and Army*. He also advocated scenes illustrating Irish social life, which
could be taken, he said, from the Poor Reports, the stories of the popular writers
Banim, Carleton or Griffin, 'or better still from observation'.

Subjects from Davis's list do crop up, both among existing paintings and in
exhibition catalogues. This may be because of his influence, but it may equally be
because he was influenced in his choice by artists he knew, and by ideas current
at the time. There is a scattering of Irish subject pictures in the annual exhibitions
of the Royal Hibernian Academy in the years before he published his suggestions.
Few of them are historical, however: on the whole they are either scenes of peasant
life or landscapes with or without ruins. On the other hand, an analysis of oil paintings exhibited annually at the Royal Hibernian Academy from its first exhibition
in 1826 until 1856 shows a sharp increase in Irish historical subjects in the early 1840s.
None of them is taken directly from Davis's list, but many are closely related to
it. (If no location is given, a picture is untraced.)[10]

Joseph Peacock (*c.* 1783–1837) exhibited at the Royal Academy, London, in 1817 a painting entitled *The Patron, or Festival of St Kevin at the Seven Churches, Glenda-* 18 *lough* (Ulster Museum, Belfast), a huge panoramic view of the valley and ruins of Glendalough, with the rather unseemly goings-on of a fairground in their midst. In 1828 he sent to the Royal Hibernian Academy a picture called *An Irish Harper singing the Legends of his Country to the Peasantry.*

Richard Rothwell (1800–1868) emigrated to London in 1829 and was, at first,

extremely successful. It was of him that Landseer said, 'An artist has come from Dublin who paints flesh as well as the Old Masters.' He exhibited several canvases of the picturesque peasant sort at the Royal Hibernian Academy in its early years – *An Irish Peasant Boy and Dog* in 1826, *Peasant Girl of Avondale* in 1827, *Kate Kearney* in 1835. Later, he showed at the British Institution *A Study from Nature: Scene, an Irish Village with its Convent, its Castle and its Hovels* in 1851, and in 1863 *The Rale [real] Colleen* 'we all have seen her in the pantomime'.

Joseph Patrick Haverty (1794–1864) was a portrait painter who occasionally did subject pieces. He showed *A Peasant's Marriage* at the Royal Hibernian Academy in 1828, but later turned to modern historical subjects like the ones on Davis's list. His picture *Advocates in a Good Cause* (National Gallery of Ireland, Dublin), in which Father Mathew is shown speaking to a repentant drunk, with the man's wife and child looking on, was exhibited at the RHA in 1846. *The Nation* review of the exhibition, on 11 July, commented: 'There is a fine pathos, too, in "Advocates in a Good Cause", a temperance scene, where wife and child are seconding our living apostle's words. In the wife's lineaments and expression especially, a whole domestic tragedy is legible.' In 1843 Haverty did a drawing, which was lithographed, of O'Connell's Monster Meeting at Clifden. In 1847 he exhibited a picture entitled *The late Daniel O'Connell Esq., reading the Manuscript of his address to the electors of Clare (Tuesday, June 24th 1828) to P. Vincent Fitzpatrick, and Frederick W. Conway, Esqrs., Painted for Mr O'Connell for presentation to Mr Fitzpatrick*. This, presumably, had been painted many years earlier.

Members of the prolific and talented Mulvany family also painted Irish subjects. Thomas J. Mulvany (1779–1845) showed *Peasants 'performing stations' at the Upper Lake of Glendalough, Co. Wicklow* in 1829. He also exhibited *The Outcast*, a subject from Oliver Goldsmith's *Deserted Village*. (Goldsmith does not figure in Davis's list, naturally, as only his nationality would give such a subject an Irish connection. Paintings illustrating his work are, however, fairly common in the mid-century,

20

19 Joseph Patrick Haverty: *O'Connell and his contemporaries: the Clare Election, 1838* (detail), perhaps an alternative version of the subject that Haverty exhibited in 1847. The excitement at O'Connell's overwhelming victory helped to carry Catholic Emancipation in 1829.

20 Joseph Patrick Haverty: *Advocates in a Good Cause*, shown in 1846.

21 Henry MacManus: *Reading 'The Nation'* (National Gallery of Ireland). The hooded cloak of the woman on the left and the Gothic arch in the background suggest that the scene is in Munster, outside the chapel after Mass on Sunday, when the paper was often read and discussed.

and Dublin honoured him with a statue, by Foley, in 1863.) In 1845 George F. Mulvany (1809–69), son of Thomas J., exhibited *St Patrick Baptizing Aengus, King of Munster* at the RHA. The catalogue entry was accompanied by the note, 'While St Patrick blessed the King, the point of his crozier was driven into the King's foot': 58 the legend tells that the King thought that this was part of the ceremony, and said nothing. The painting was bought by the Royal Irish Art Union, and was won as a prize by Lord Talbot de Malahide. It once hung in the Catholic church at Malahide.

Henry MacManus (*c.* 1810–78) is a painter who was much more clearly connected with the patriotic movements of his time than any other whom we have discussed so far, except perhaps Henry O'Neill. He came from Monaghan, and was a friend of Gavan Duffy, a fellow townsman.[11] Association with members of the Young Ireland group converted him from being an Orangeman to a nationalist sympathizer. He painted portraits of Dillon, MacNevin and Davis (the only contemporary portrait of him), and several of O'Connell. He helped Gavan Duffy design the cap which was presented to O'Connell in 1843 (of which more later). He sent *The Irish* 22 *Assizes* and *Donnybrook Fair* to the RHA in 1838, and in 1840 *The Midnight Mass*, a subject from Carleton's *Traits and Stories*. This last was a source later suggested by Davis. In 1842 he showed *O'Donoghue's Mistress, a Legend of Killarney*, accompanied by an explanation in the catalogue:

> There was a young and beautiful girl, whose imagination was so impressed with the idea of the visionary chieftain that she fancied herself in love with him, and at last, in a fit of insanity, on a May morning, threw herself into the lake.

The subject was from Thomas Moore, and was later used by Daniel Maclise. At the Dublin Exhibition of 1853 and the RHA of 1854 MacManus showed *The Introduction of Christianity into Ireland*, which was accompanied in the 1853 catalogue by a long passage about the origin of the shamrock, St Patrick's dispute with the Druids, and so on.[12] MacManus's best-known picture is *Reading 'The Nation'*, which 21 shows an old man reading the paper, surrounded by a group of intent people listening and arguing.

Nicholas J. Crowley (1819–57), who specialized in conversation pieces, also went in a lot for specifically Irish subjects. In 1840 he showed at the RHA *Sudden Appearance of Richard Nugent Baron, of Dublin, before King James I* – a subject taken, the catalogue tells us, from the *History of England*, though it doesn't say which. In 1845 he exhibited a portrait of O'Connell, painted during his imprisonment, and *The Banshee*, and in 1848 *The Desmond Bride*, illustrating a story in which the heir to the Earl of Desmond, having married the daughter of a peasant, is rejected by his family and clan.

Bernard Mulrenin (1803–68) also turned his hand to Irish subjects, though he was mainly a painter of miniatures, among them portraits of O'Curry, O'Donovan, Petrie, and Sir William and Lady Wilde. In 1845 he exhibited at the RHA *Gráinne* 13 *Maol carrying off the Infant Heir of Howth*. Gráinne Maol, or Grace O'Malley, was a female pirate who, finding the gates of Howth Castle locked against her, kidnapped the heir, and only returned him on condition that a place was always laid for her at table and the gates never locked at dinnertime. The catalogue entry, which does not give a source, describes her: 'Her hair was gathered on the top of her head, and fastened with a golden bodkin. She wore a yellow dress, and was covered with a large and flowing scarlet mantle.' In 1846 Mulrenin showed a picture called *Fionn-ghuala*. While this may have been immediately inspired by Thomas Moore's poem, 'The Song of Fionnuala', it is remarkable as an example of subject-matter taken from Irish mythology, from the cycles of stories which tell of Fionn and of Oisín, of Cuchulainn and Queen Maeve. Though these stories were known, and had already appeared in translation in the eighteenth century, and were used in poetry by people like Ferguson, they seem not to have been attractive to painters, whose favourite subjects were historical, or pseudo-historical, as in the case of St Patrick and the shamrock.

Although it has been possible, by carefully looking through exhibition catalogues and existing paintings, to assemble a body of Irish subject pictures, it should be remembered that these are by no means representative. The bulk of the exhibits might as readily have been seen in London, Birmingham, or Edinburgh. There was no coherent body of Irish art distinguishable by its subject or by its style. Some painters, not usually of the first rank, were impelled by patriotic motives. Others may well have chosen subjects like *O'Donoghue's Mistress* or *The Desmond Bride* as the local equivalent of popular Victorian subjects like *Ophelia* or *King Cophetua and the Beggar Maid*. As far as painting was concerned, Davis, though he may have had some slight contemporary influence, had no deeply lasting effect. The catalogue to the Dublin Exhibition of 1853 has an interesting explanation for this poverty of Irish art: 'among a free people, which feels and knows itself free, there only Art takes root and prospers: remove the political Life and Art also languishes and dies'; 'the condition of a helpless province has been found to be here . . . fatal to the progress of Art.'[13]

It was not only in the pages of *The Nation* that Davis and his friends pursued the cause of Irish art: they also did their best to awaken the Repeal Association, and began with the cards of membership. According to Gavan Duffy,[14]

> The cards of membership for all O'Connell's associations had been as bare of sentiment as the price list of a commercial traveller; under the influence of the young poets new cards were issued which became a sort of diploma of political rank, and blossomed into poetry and history.

Once again Gavan Duffy is putting the Young Ireland achievement a bit high. At the time the cards may have seemed to 'blossom', but to the modern eye they are rather dry. They were simply early in the field with what are by now well worn clichés of national imagery. One shows the Parliament House in College Green, with a sunburst behind it, and the date 1782, the year in which the Irish Parliament achieved comparative legislative freedom, and consequently an important date for the Repeal movement and for Young Ireland. Another card shows a map of Ireland, with the legends 'God save the Queen' and 'Ireland for the Irish'. The most elaborate has an ornate crocketted Gothic frame, with inset portraits of O'Connell, Grattan 16 and Flood in the central arch, and figures from Irish history, ancient and modern (including Sarsfield, Owen Roe O'Neill, Brian Boroimhe or Boru and Ollamh Fodhla), in the flanking ones. A trophy group in the centre shows a harp against a sunburst, and sword, shield, cap and horn in a wreath of shamrock.

The Repeal Association had a scheme to offer prizes for pictures and sculpture of Irish historical subjects treated in a national spirit, and for engravings and lithographs from 'national pictures'. The idea was to replace the 'rude and sometimes

22 *The Uncrowned Monarch's first Levee*: O'Connell wearing the 'Milesian crown' and the uniform of the Eighty Two Club, deferred to by a representative of British power – *Punch*'s view, reproduced by Gavan Duffy in *Young Ireland*.

indecent daubs' in cabins and lodgings by things well-drawn and of national inter-est.[15] Prizes were also offered for designs for Catholic, Protestant, and Presbyterian churches, and for public buildings, though it is not clear what, if anything, came of this. Local representatives of the Association, known as Repeal Wardens, were urged to watch over historic ruins in their districts. Again, it is not clear to what extent this scheme worked. Throughout the century there were constant complaints as to the state of historic monuments, and nothing very organized was done until the setting up of the national monuments section of the Board of Works after the disestablishment of the Church of Ireland in 1869 (see below, p. 64).

The attempts of the Association at a reform in dress were more comical than anything else. One idea was to gain acceptance for a hat of characteristically Irish design to replace the varieties commonly worn, especially, no doubt, the *caubeen* so familiar from the pages of *Punch*. Duffy, whose idea it was, enlisted the help of Henry MacManus, and between them they designed a cap based on the Milesian crown. (The Milesians, according to the twelfth-century *Book of Invasions*, were the ancestors of the modern Irish.) It had a stiff border, shaped like a crown, and a 'jellybag' tasselled centre. A version was made of green velvet, the border embroidered in gold with shamrocks, and presented to Daniel O'Connell, with considerable ceremony, by the sculptor John Hogan and the painter MacManus, at the Monster Meeting at Mullaghmast in 1843. It looked well, Duffy tells us, on

52

the commanding forehead of The Liberator, and did not want a certain antique dignity.[16] In the common version, made of grey shoddy, and 'relieved by a feeble wreath of green shamrocks', it 'bore an awkward and fatal resemblance to a night-cap', and did not become popular. O'Connell, however, wore his. Its similarity to a crown was seized upon by hostile observers, the interpretation being that O'Connell had been offered, and accepted, the Crown of Ireland. *Punch* fell on this with great glee, and published a cartoon, *The Uncrowned Monarch's first Levee*, which 22 shows O'Connell wearing the cap. It is also sometimes used in *Punch* cartoons of the period on the heads of murderous-looking thugs with low foreheads and heavy jaws, as an indication, if any were needed, that they were Irish.

Another excursion into fancy-dress was the uniform of the Eighty Two Club.[17] This was set up in 1844, with O'Connell as President. Its declared object was to encourage Irish art and literature, and to diffuse national feeling through society. Its first public banquet was held on the sixty-third anniversary of the day in 1782 when Grattan made his speech calling for Irish freedom. At it Davis was called upon to propose a toast connected with the arts in Ireland. The club had an expensive uniform, two examples of which survive in the National Museum of Ireland, that which belonged to Davis, and William Smith O'Brien's. They have the familiar shape of dress uniforms – jacket short and tight in front, with a stand-up collar, 22 and narrow, braided trousers. They are made of green fabric, with shamrocks embroidered in gold on collar and cuffs, and shamrock-embossed gold buttons. It was not until much later in the century that the kilt, with a *brat*, a rectangle of fabric held at the shoulder by a 'Tara'-type brooch, began to be adopted as patriotic dress (see p. 148).

CHAPTER 4

Painting, sculpture and architecture

As we have seen, though there was no distinctly Irish school of art in the mid-nineteenth century, national feeling manifested itself in various degrees among artists working at home. Similarly, among those who had successful careers abroad, especially in England, Irish subject-matter and, in some cases, patriotic feeling, did appear. Nostalgia for Ireland's period of glory, the early Middle Ages, was strengthened by a tendency in Europe as a whole to look to the medieval period for subject-matter or style, expressed in the Gothic and allied revivals. There was also a growing interest in more exotic contemporary scenes – North Africa and the Middle East, of course, but also the less trodden corners at home, Brittany, Scotland, the West of Ireland. This makes it difficult to decide, in the case of Irish artists, to what extent we are dealing with patriotic fervour and to what extent with fashionable archaeological or sociological interest, or even a taste for picturesque peasants and a distaste for urban industrial society.

This problem arises in considering the work of Frederic Burton. As we have seen, he was closely linked with the antiquarians, made drawings for Petrie, knew Wilde and Stokes and Ferguson, O'Donovan and O'Curry. He was on the Council and on the Committee of Antiquities of the Royal Irish Academy, and one of the founders of the Irish Archaeological Society. He was also a close friend of Thomas Davis, even to the extent of designing (albeit anonymously) the frontispiece for the first edition of *The Spirit of the Nation* in 1845. This book became a symbol of nationalism for succeeding generations, and he was teased about it in later life by Lady Gregory. 'It was Davis who asked me to do it,' he explained, 'and there was nothing I could refuse Davis.'[1] Davis and his circle had high hopes of Burton as founder of a national school of painting. He was in fact a staunch Unionist, left Ireland in his thirty-fifth year after his mother died, and seems not to have had much to do with it after he settled in London. On the other hand, he must have had a fairly strong interest in and feeling for the country to be so integrated a part of the Dublin circle in which he moved. He treated his Irish subjects with great sympathy. Unlike Daniel Maclise, who was much more emotionally patriotic, he never descended to caricatures of ape-like Irishmen: on the contrary, he idealized them. The blind peasant girl in *The Blind Girl at the Holy Well* (exhibited at the RHA in 1840, engraved for the Royal Irish Art Union in the same year, and since destroyed) was not an authentic peasant, as her dress and bare feet would suggest, but one of Petrie's daughters. Lady Gregory explained this many years later by saying that for Burton no type could be too refined or too delicate for the idealized Irish peasant who did not understand himself.[2] This may be the explanation, though

17
3

24

23 Daniel Maclise: detail of *Snap-apple night, or All-Hallow Eve, in Ireland*, shown in 1833. The woman in the left foreground wears a shawl celebrating O'Connell. On the right a man 'snaps' at an apple. The picture is said to include the portraits of Father Horgan and Crofton Croker: see p. 44.

24 Frederic Burton: *The Blind Girl at the Holy Well*, engraved by H. T. Ryall in 1840.

it smacks of the patriotism of 1916 rather than that of 1840. Burton's *Aran Fisher- 25 man's Drowned Child* (RHA 1841, RA 1842, engraved for the Royal Irish Art Union 1843) is typical of its period in its obvious emotion and the exaggerated drama of its gestures. Individual faces, however, are treated delicately and sympathetically. The details of costume and the inside of the cabin have been carefully studied, obviously from life, with the same accuracy and attention to detail he would put into an antiquarian sketch to send to Petrie. Only the gestures have been dramatized in the picture, and the costumes and interior have not, apparently, been glamorized.

25 Frederic Burton:
*The Aran Fisherman's
Drowned Child*,
watercolour, *c.* 1841
(National Gallery
of Ireland). The
antiquarians who were
Burton's friends were
very interested in the
language, customs and
music of the islands.

These pictures, which were among the most popular that the Art Union produced, were done by Burton during the early part of his career, when he was in
daily contact with the leaders of the antiquarian movement. In 1851 he left Ireland,
and spent several years in Germany before settling in London. In 1874 he was made,
to everyone's surprise, Director of the National Gallery, and after that he ceased
to paint. This seems a pity, for he was a superb artist, one of the best that Ireland
or indeed England produced in the nineteenth century, even though he only painted
in watercolours.

Another important Irish painter in exile, ten years older than Burton, was Daniel Maclise (1806–70), but in his case the paintings which demonstrate his preoccupation with Ireland occur during the later part of his career in England.[3] He was born in Cork, of Scottish descent, and had his art training in the recently-established Cork School of Art. The success of Cork in producing artists of the calibre of Maclise and the sculptor John Hogan has been attributed to its possession of a famous set of casts from the antique. These had been taken from statues in the Vatican under [33] the supervision of Canova, and presented by Pope Pius VII to George IV, then Prince Regent, in gratitude for England's part in the Napoleonic Wars. They reached London in 1818, and were left lying around the London Custom House 'performing a kind of ignoble quarantine in their unopened cases'. Eventually they were put in the Tent Room in the gardens of Carlton House, where they were in the way. The Prince tried to present them to the Royal Academy, which claimed it had no room. Eventually Lord Ennismore obtained them for Cork. There they formed the basis of the early art training of students, among then Maclise.[4]

Maclise also became acquainted, as a young man, with a group of men interested in antiquities and folklore. They included Richard Sainthill, an antiquarian who returned to live in Cork in 1821. He was an early patron and friend, introducing Maclise to other antiquarians and encouraging his work. Maclise later said of him that he was a gentleman 'whose antiquarian knowledge and various literary attainments eminently qualified him for inspiring a youth with a devotion to the classic, to the sublime, and to the beautiful', and that he directed the young artist's attention to 'medalling, to heraldry and the like exercises'.[5] Another friend was Thomas Crofton Croker (1798–1854), author of *Fairy Legends and Traditions of the South of Ireland*, a pioneer work in the study of folklore. Maclise did some illustrations for the second edition which appeared in 1826. It was Croker who took Maclise to visit Father Horgan, parish priest of Blarney, a man interested in antiquities and [41] famous for his hospitality – a visit on which Maclise based his picture *Snap-apple* [23] *night, or All-Hallow Eve, in Ireland*, exhibited at the Royal Academy in 1833 (now in a private collection).[6] The painting includes portraits of Father Horgan and of Croker, so diminutive a man that he was known to his friends as 'The Honourable Member for Fairyland'.

Maclise himself was interested in Irish antiquities, and there are numbers of sketches of architectural remains which he made on various walking tours in his youth. On his way back to Cork from a visit to Dublin in the summer of 1826, he made drawings of Cashel, neighbouring Hore Abbey, Holy Cross, and other [26] sites.[7] This was not really unusual: topographical art was one of the basic branches of the profession. Dozens of artists made studies of Irish architectural remains, and many earned a living by it. More unusual are the studies Maclise made, later in life, of various pieces of Celtic jewellery. There is a sketchbook of his in the Victoria and Albert Museum, London (which also possesses many of his early topographical drawings), possibly dating from the 1850s, that is full of drawings of ancient ornaments with notes about their provenance – a sketch of a ring-brooch marked '4½ inches diametre, found in Co. Roscommon'; another ring-brooch 'in possession of J. C. Croker', two fibulae 'dug up near Brahalish, Bantry, Co. Cork', and many more. They are evidence of Maclise's continuing interest in, and study of, Irish antiquities.

The circle in which Maclise moved in London, that of the contributors to *Fraser's Magazine*, included a large proportion of Irishmen, among them three fellow Corkmen, Croker, William Maginn and Francis Mahony (alias Father Prout, author of *The Bells of Shandon*). He was also, according to Gavan Duffy, member of an 'Irish Society' in London, an extension of the Young Ireland movement at home.[8]

Maclise's most full-blooded and best-known Irish picture is his *Marriage of Strongbow and Eva*, officially *Richard de Clare, Earl of Pembroke, surnamed Strongbow ... Receives the hand of the Princess Eva, from her father, Dermot Mac Murrogh, King of Leinster, in fulfilment of his compact with that lord, and with promise of succession to his throne*, exhibited at the Royal Academy in 1854. The catalogue entry is accompanied by a long description of the event:[9]

> The marriage ceremony was solemnized on the battle field, after the siege of the sacked and ruined city of Waterford, and it was in the midst of its scenes of desolation that the conqueror received the hand of the Princess Eva; at which time, as the chronicler relates, 'The famous Strongbow did not celebrate his particular wedding-day, but the indissoluble knot of the Irish allegiance to the English souvcraignetie, with the same ring which circuled his wive's finger, affiancing that island to this our country.'

Maclise was requested by the Commissioners of Fine Arts to reproduce the scene for a compartment in the Conference Hall of the Houses of Parliament at Westminster, 'the subject being selected by us for that apartment'. On the face of it, the subject was a suitable one: it has the same kind of reference to Ireland's subjugation to England as Waldré's *Henry II meeting the Irish Leaders*. Maclise's treatment of it, however, was more sympathetic to Ireland than to England. The scene is sacrificial, not festive or simply solemn: the bride's head is bowed more in submission than in modesty, and the groom's martial foot is planted on a fallen cross ornamented with Celtic interlace. The marriage is taking place against the background

45

27, 28 Daniel Maclise:
*The Marriage of
Strongbow and Eva,*
shown in 1854
(National Gallery of
Ireland). The figure of
the bard, symbol for
Maclise of the Celts'
departed glory, holds a
harp similar to that of
Brian Boru (ill. 6).

of a series of entombment scenes, and the foreground is a writing mass of dead, dying, and captive warriors. Among them is a bard with a harp, apparently a symbol for Maclise of the departed greatness of the Celt. Maclise's archaeological studies are apparent from an engraved stone slab in the foreground, inscribed with the Irish words *oroit do mac* (pray for mac . . .), and also from the interlace ornament on the bard's harp and on the costumes of the fallen warriors. This is not to say, however, that the picture as a whole is historically exact. Though individual details have been carefully studied, they have been mixed together with a certain disregard for period, and the painting was criticized for such inaccuracy in the *Art Journal* review of the Royal Academy exhibition.[10] Nevertheless the review praised it as 'a truly great work', and encouraged its selection for Westminster while recognizing its inconsistency as propaganda:

> In order to account for the solemnization of this marriage under such circumstances, it should have been stated in the catalogue that it was a necessity. Strongbow was wedded to his wife in his battle panoply and sword in hand, because the news had arrived that Dublin was in revolt.

Maclise also drew on the *Irish Melodies* of Thomas Moore, a very popular source of iconography for Irish art in the nineteenth century. Moore provided an abundance of Irish sentiment, cast in a romantic mould, but toned down, and made respectable – Hazlitt said of him that he converted the wild harp of Erin into a musical snuff-box.[11] Moore and Maclise were friends, and Maclise illustrated the Longman

The origin of the Harp.

'Tis believ'd that this Harp, which I wake now
for thee,
Was a Siren of old, who sung under the sea;
And who often, at eve, thro' the bright waters rov'd,
To meet, on the green shore, a youth whom she lov'd.

But she lov'd him in vain, for he left her to weep,
And in tears, all the night her gold tresses to steep;
Till heav'n look'd with pity on true-love so warm,
And chang'd to this soft Harp the sea-maiden's form.

D. Maclise R.A.   W. Taylor

edition of the *Irish Melodies* in 1845. Moore wrote in the Preface that he deemed it most fortunate that the rich imaginative powers of Mr Maclise had been employed in its adornment, and that 'to complete its national character an Irish pencil has lent its aid to an Irish pen in rendering due honour and homage to our country's ancient harp'. Maclise's painting *The Origin of the Harp*, exhibited at the Royal Academy in 1842, is based on one of the songs, of the same name, in the collection. Moore himself had got the subject from Edward Hudson, whom he had visited in Kilmainham Gaol after his involvement in the rebellion of 1798. To pass the time, Hudson had made a large drawing on the wall of his cell, representing the fancied origin of the Irish harp. The poem ends:[12]

> Still her bosom rose fair – still her cheeks smil'd the same –
> While her sea-beauties gracefully form'd the light frame;
> And her hair, as, let loose, o'er her white arm it fell,
> Was chang'd to bright chords, utt'ring melody's spell.

Another subject Maclise took from Moore was *O'Donoghue's Mistress*, a theme which had earlier been treated by Henry MacManus, and exhibited at the RHA in 1842. Davis said that Maclise had taken the best poetical subject from Moore, and did not advise anyone to compete with him.[13] Curiously enough, Maclise's last oil, exhibited at the RA in 1870, *The Earls of Desmond and Ormond*, was one of the subjects suggested by Davis thirty years earlier under the title *Kildare 'on the necks of the Butlers'*. The story, taken from Leland's history, is of a battle between the Earl of Desmond (Fitzgerald – Kildare was another family title) and the Earl of Ormond (Butler). Desmond was defeated and carried off the battlefield by the victorious Butlers, who taunted him: '"Where now is the great Earl of Desmond?" "In his proper place," retorted the Geraldine, witty as he was wild; "on the necks of the Butlers!"'[14]

Maclise is the most renowned Irish painter of the nineteenth century, and deservedly so, for he worked on a heroic scale. His draughtsmanship was superb, both in his early portrait drawings and in his later paintings. He could not always handle large compositions, however. *The Marriage of Strongbow and Eva* is very scrappy in its organization and requires concentration from the viewer. His emotionalism, influenced as it was by German Romantic painting, is sometimes overpowering, whether he was dealing with Irish subject-matter or with scenes from English history or literature, which he treated even more frequently.

The third major Irish painter to make a name for himself abroad in the mid-nineteenth century was William Mulready (1786–1863). He was the son of a leather breeches maker from Ennis, Co. Clare. He left the country when he was about six, and does not seem to have had much connection with it subsequently, though he did send pictures to Irish exhibitions, and was regarded in Ireland as an Irish artist. The nearest he ever comes to Irish subject-matter is in illustrating the work of an Irish author, Oliver Goldsmith, both in a published edition and in a series of paintings from *The Vicar of Wakefield*, so his Irish link is very tenuous indeed.

The same is true of the sculptor Patrick MacDowell (1799–1870). He was born in Belfast, but his widowed mother emigrated to England when he was eleven or twelve. He did a monument to the Marchioness of Donegall, and statues of the Earl of Belfast for his native city and of the Earl of Eglinton and Winton for Dublin, but there do not seem to be any Irish themes among his subject pieces.

29 Daniel Maclise: illustration of 'The Origin of the Harp', from Thomas Moore's *Irish Melodies*, 1845.

John Henry Foley (1818–74) has slightly stronger links with Ireland. He was born in Dublin, and got his art education in the Schools of the Royal Dublin Society, which he entered in 1831. He was sixteen when he left Ireland in 1834. His subsequent career in England was extremely successful, and he became a leading maker of monuments, a position which was consecrated by his being chosen, after the elimination of Baron Marochetti, to do the statue of the Prince Consort for the Albert Memorial in Kensington Gardens, London. Ireland is littered with monuments by him, though there is nothing particularly significant in that – so is England, and he did statues for places as far afield as Calcutta (Viscount Hardinge, Sir James Outram), Bombay (Lord Elphinstone, Manochjee Nesserwanjee), and Lexington, Virginia (General Jackson). Among his Dublin statues are Goldsmith (1863) and Burke (1868) outside Trinity College, and Henry Grattan (1874) in College Green, 30 put up to forestall a monument to the Prince Consort, which was eventually sited elsewhere. He did the statue of Father Mathew for Cork, unveiled on 10 October 1864, the anniversary of the birth of that apostle of temperance.[15] His most significant Dublin monument from the national point of view is the O'Connell 32 Monument in Sackville (now, of course, O'Connell) Street.[16]

O'Connell had died in 1847, and work was in hand to commemorate him by a memorial in the form of a round tower in Glasnevin Cemetery (see below, pp. 58–60). Some time later is was felt that he should also have a monument in Dublin City, and in 1862 a subscription list was opened, though the form of the monument had not been decided. Two years later, in 1864, it was decided to hold a competition for a design, the selection committee including, besides dignitaries like the Lord Chancellor of Ireland and the President of the Royal Hibernian Academy, George Petrie, Frederic Burton and William Stokes. There were sixty entries for the competition, including seven models which were described in detail in *The Irish Builder* on 15 February 1865. James Cahill (d. 1890) submitted a design with an octagonal base and radiating pedestals with figures of St Patrick, Brian Boroimhe, Ollamh Fodhla and Ossian. The intervals were to have bas reliefs showing events from O'Connell's life. Above was an architectural composition of the Corinthian order, with figures of Erin, Faith, Liberty and Charity, and the four provinces of Ireland. On top was O'Connell, wrapped in the well-known cloak (though it was later claimed that he rarely wore one). The design proposed by John Farrell (1829–1901) had a statue of O'Connell (which *The Irish Builder* scornfully described as 'Mr Foley's Caractacus in a frock-coat'), surrounded by Eloquence, Patriotism, Unanimity and Peace. The submission by Thomas Turner (d. 1892) also had a statue of O'Connell ('a Virginian negro in a night shirt') and figures representing each of the four provinces under the protection of its patron saint. The committee found nothing to its liking in all of this, and withheld the premiums. A second competition was held, for which twenty designs were submitted, but once again the committee found itself unable to recommend any of the designs. They were all 'wanting in grandeur and simplicity'.[17] It decided to invite John Henry Foley to do the figure of O'Connell, and resident Irish artists subsidiary figures. Foley declined to have anything to do with it unless the whole scheme was entrusted to him. Eventually, after further dithering, the committee decided to do so.

Indignation, which had been simmering in Dublin since the results of the first competition were announced, boiled over, and continued to do so while Foley got

30 John Henry Foley: bronze monument to Henry Grattan, 1874, sited opposite the old Parliament House in Dublin where Grattan had spoken so often.

down to the business of designing the monument. Foley, it was said, was an absentee artist 'who has been so absorbed by the wealth and blandishments of Babylon that his native land seems to be to him a thing of nought'. The committee might feel that it was fulfilling its obligations to the country by giving the commission to a London sculptor, Irish by birth. But this was putting a premium on artist absentee-ism, and furthermore was spending money subscribed in Ireland, abroad. Besides, Foley had a great deal of work on hand – the Albert Memorial, Lord Rosse, Lord Gough, Benjamin Lee Guinness. During his visit to Ireland he had got a fresh commission, a statue of Lord Dunkellin for Galway. In short, 'genius may be over-worked in London, while it is overlooked in Dublin at the same moment'.[18] These criticisms were not entirely unjustified: work on the O'Connell Monument dragged on, and it was still incomplete when Foley died in 1874, having caught a chill, it was said, sitting on damp clay modelling the bust of the Asia figure for the Albert Memorial. The O'Connell Monument was completed by his assistant, Thomas Brock.

31 Christopher Moore:
bronze monument to
Thomas Moore in
Dublin, 1857.

The monument is in three parts. At the base are four winged victories, Patriotism
with a sword and shield, Fidelity with an Irish wolfhound, Courage and Eloquence.
Above this, round a drum, is a frieze on the theme of O'Connell's labours. The
central figure is Erin, a harp beside her and a wreath of shamrock in her hair. Her
right hand points up to O'Connell, and her left holds the Act of Catholic Emancipation. She is trampling on her broken fetters. The monument is topped by the cloaked
figure of O'Connell. As a composition it lacks the urbanity of Foley's other work
in Dublin. The drum in particular is crowded and awkwardly composed, and at
least one of the figures looks in danger of losing its precarious foothold on the plinth.

Christopher Moore (1790–1863) was another expatriate Irish sculptor, like Foley
a Dubliner settled in London. He was at his best in portrait busts, but, as Gavan
Duffy put it, 'proved on trial to be unequal to statues'.[19] His monument to Thomas
Moore, in College Street, Dublin, has deservedly been an object of derision ever
since it was put up in 1857. Indeed, it was one of the criticisms of the bungling
O'Connell Monument Committee that some of its members had been on the committee for the Moore statue: *The Irish Builder* on 15 September 1865 scolded, 'And
what are we to say of the high artistic taste of some of the members of this O'Connell
award committee who on a former occasion gave their decision in favour of that
hideous importation from London, the Moore Statue . . .' – a decision, it went on
to say, which broke the heart of John Hogan.

32 John Henry Foley:
monument to Daniel
O'Connell in Dublin,
of bronze and stone,
1864–82. This detail of
the base shows Fidelity,
with an Irish
wolfhound; above her
is Erin, pointing up
towards O'Connell.

Of the leading Irish sculptors of the nineteenth century Hogan (1800–1858) is the one most closely associated with national sentiments.[20] He was born at Tallow, Co. Waterford, but at the age of sixteen was apprenticed to Thomas Deane, the architect, in Cork. Like Maclise, his art education was stimulated by the collection of casts from antique models in the Royal Cork Institution. His sculptural skills soon attracted attention, and money was collected to send him to Rome in 1824. He remained there, except for occasional visits to Ireland, until his final return, with his wife and six children, in 1849. He was plainly highly thought of there: Thorvaldsen is said to have remarked, on leaving the city, that Hogan was the best sculptor he left behind him in Rome, and in 1837 he was elected a member of the Virtuosi del Pantheon, an honour which had not, until then, been conferred on any 'British' artist. His doings were frequently reported in *The Nation*. It is interesting to note that exile in Rome was not considered in at all the same light as exile in London. It was presumably on his visits home that he became acquainted with the men of Young Ireland, and he seems to have actively kept up a connection with his country:

33 A storeroom in the School of Art at Cork: in the right foreground are two sculptures by Hogan (a *Dead Christ* and *The Drunken Faun*), in the background an Andrew O'Connor (see p. 186) and some of the casts from the antique (including the Belvedere torso, Laocoon and cymbal-playing satyr) that played so important a part in the education of Cork artists such as Hogan and Maclise.

34 John Hogan:
monument to James
Doyle, Bishop of
Kildare and Leighlin,
in Carlow Cathedral;
marble, won in
competition in 1837
and completed in
Rome in 1839.

when Samuel Ferguson set out for Rome in 1845 Petrie gave him a letter of introduction to Hogan.[21] Davis called him, along with Maclise, one of the '*present* glories
of Cork',[22] and he headed the deputation which gave the 'Milesian crown' to
O'Connell. In the *Irish Penny Journal* of 19 December 1840 Petrie dealt in detail
with Hogan's monument to James Doyle, Bishop of Kildare and Leighlin (known, 34
because of his episcopal signature, as JKL). We see, he wrote,

> a Christian prelate in the act of offering up a last appeal to heaven for the regeneration
> of his country, which is personified by a beautiful female figure, who is represented
> in an attitude of dejection at his side ... In the figure of the prostrate female we recognise
> at a glance the attributes of our country ... She is represented as resting on one knee,
> her body bent and humbled, yet in her majestic form retaining a fullness of beauty
> and dignity of character; her turret crowned head resting on one arm, while the other,
> with an expression of melancholy abandonment, reclines on and sustains her ancient
> harp. In the male figure who stands behind her in an attitude of the most unaffected grace
> and dignity, we see a personification of the sublime in the Episcopal character. He stands
> erect, his enthusiastic and deeply intellectual countenance directed upwards imploringly,
> while with one hand he touches with delicate affection his earthly mistress, and with
> the other stretched forth with passionate devotion, he appeals to heaven for her
> protection.

Hogan seems to have specialized in figures accompanied by Erin. His *Erin with a Bust of Lord Cloncurry* (Lyons House, Co. Kildare) was exhibited at the Cork Exhibition of 1852 and in Dublin in 1853, where it was praised in the catalogue as 'a grander and nobler work than any we have mentioned . . . a figure which might well adorn the Hall of an Irish National Gallery'. Another similar group, which he only executed in plaster, *Erin with Brian Boru* (Crawford Municipal Art Gallery, Cork), shows his familiar Erin, with harp and castellated crown, flanked by a naked small boy, his foot on a wolfhound.

As we have seen, Hogan made a design for the Moore Monument, an elegant little model in plaster. He was defeated in the competition by Christopher Moore – 'with what wisdom and justice subsequent events have shown', said *The Irish Builder* in 1859, 'to our perpetual national disgrace'.[23] Hogan's career as a sculptor was indeed much less successful than his talent deserved. He was no less accomplished than Foley or MacDowell, but did not manage to achieve their eminence. He was even defeated in the competition for the Moore statue by a sculptor considerably his inferior. Perhaps his politics were against him, or perhaps his religion. He was a Catholic and indeed made some of the best religious sculpture Ireland has seen.

Whatever the vicissitudes of painters and sculptors, architects, at least, had no difficulty in keeping going. There was a vigorous and busy native profession, notwithstanding the fact that many important commissions went to English architects. Irish architects who had successes abroad, for example Benjamin Woodward and W. H. Lynn, remained resident in Ireland. Since one of the phenomena of nineteenth-century architecture, in Ireland as in England, was the revival of medieval styles, it was natural that architects should look at ancient Irish architecture. On the whole, however, the pattern of the revival was the same as in England, with architects looking at English Norman and French Romanesque, and English, French, German and Italian Gothic. The architects who looked to Irish models were exceptional.

As was the case with the other arts, specifically Irish connections in architecture are to be found earlier than the flowering of the Irish revival in the 1840s. The Irish followers of Wyatt and Adam in the late eighteenth century had adopted the Irish style of crenellation, with double-stepped battlements, as more picturesque than the English, and made it a feature of the Irish castle style. Francis Johnston (1760–1829), who sometimes designed in a Gothick style, used the same type of battlement, for example at Charleville Castle, Co. Offaly (begun in 1801), and at Markree, Co. Sligo.[24] In ecclesiastical architecture, as Maurice Craig has pointed out, there is a resemblance between the parabolic stone vault of John Semple's Black Church in Dublin and stone-roofed Irish churches of the eleventh century.[25] Sir Richard Morrison (1767–1849), a Neo-Classical architect of the early nineteenth century, looked back to Irish Palladian architecture.[26] This is not, to be sure, a Celtic revival, but the tendency to look back to another great period of Irish history, when Ireland had an independent Parliament in Dublin, is another strand of national sentiment which must be taken into account. It is a theme which recurs throughout the nineteenth century, and into the twentieth. The membership cards of the Repeal Association show the eighteenth-century Parliament House in College Green, and portraits of the eighteenth-century statesmen Grattan and Flood. Eighteenth-century subjects figure among Davis's themes for history painters – *Grattan Moving*

35 John Hogan: competition design for a monument to Thomas Moore, plaster, c. 1857 (National Gallery of Ireland).

Liberty, Flood Apostrophizing Corruption. Samuel Ferguson was interested in Irish architectural remains, and (in a review of Thomas Mulvany's *Life of Gandon*, in 1847) inveighed against the Ecclesiastical Commissioners for their treatment of them:[27]

> not content with erecting its tasteless buildings on independent sites, this corporation employs our money and compromises our character in pulling down our most valuable historic monuments, to make room for its spurious and insignificant creations ...
>
> We deem it more the expedient of a barbarian than the policy of an educated man to destroy evidences of past civilisation in order to reconcile men to the notion that they are 'a people without a history', who ought, of right, to occupy an inferior position, and learn contentedly the lesson of dependence.

Nevertheless, he was against the revival of medieval architecture, and believed, profoundly, that classical styles were best. He expressed this feeling in verse:[28]

> Yes, Down Hill was founded
> When builders were grounded
> (Let Ruskin go lecture!)
> In sound architecture:
>
> And the men who were able
> From state-room to stable
> To roof and to wall so,
> Could found a state also.

(Down Hill, Co. Derry, was a fine house built in the 1780s for the Earl Bishop of Derry by Michael Shanahan. It is now a shell.) In his review of the *Life of Gandon*, Ferguson said that what Ireland had to boast of was her music and her architecture of the age of Independence. The music was entirely her own, but the architecture had been transplanted from England. Nevertheless the patrons 'were in feeling and affection, as well as by long naturalisation, altogether Irish, and, whether the executive ability derived from England or from Italy, the monuments themselves equally belong to the country whose liberality and taste appropriated them.' The buildings erected by Gandon had, he said, been the principal evidences of national taste and civilization to which the Irish could refer. In fact, the publication of a life of Gandon in 1846 is an indication of the growing interest in eighteenth-century Irish architecture.[29] Even Petrie, so closely linked with Ireland's other Golden Age, made studies of Dublin's Georgian buildings.

There were, naturally, a number of architectural connections among the antiquarians, and vice-versa. Sir Richard Morrison's son, William Vitruvius Morrison (1794–1838), knew Petrie, and sketched and measured buildings for him.[30] He drew the medieval church at Killeshin, Co. Laois, in 1833 'with his wonted skill and judgement', and he also made sketches and measurements of the round tower at Ratoo, Co. Kerry. An immigrant architect, George Wilkinson (*fl.* 1839–81), who designed dozens of poorhouses and railway stations in Ireland, published *Practical Geology and Ancient Architecture of Ireland* in 1845. There is not much sign of the influence of that ancient architecture in his own building.[31]

Petrie himself took a hand in an architectural project, a monument-tomb for O'Connell in Glasnevin Cemetery. A model was shown at the Dublin Exhibition of 1853: neither the drawings nor the model have yet been found, but fortunately

110

36 The O'Connell memorial round tower in Glasnevin Cemetery, Dublin, completed by 1869.

Petrie described the scheme very fully in a report to the committee for the memorial in 1851.[32] There was to be a chapel, a high cross, and a round tower. The chapel was 'in that simple and characteristic style of architecture peculiar to the earliest ages of Christianity in this country', and was therefore an exceedingly plain building, a nave with a small rectangular chancel, the walls sloping slightly inwards, with a very high pointed roof so as to give a pyramidal appearance to the composition. The west doorway was to have a flat lintel, and the east window a semicircular arch. He suggested granite as a suitable material. To this main feature were to be added a round tower belfry, standing 15 feet (about 5 metres) south of the chapel, and a high cross with very little carved ornament, so as to be consistent with the style of the other two elements. Petrie planned to place the whole group on a raised platform. He had adhered strictly, he said, to ancient examples, and endeavoured to embody the principles which appeared to have existed in the minds of the old builders. He felt that the monument

> could not fail of being interesting to all cultivated minds, as well as to country-loving Irishmen of every class and creed. For, when every vestige shall have disappeared of those ancient ecclesiastical structures in the possession of which any other nation would feel the highest national pride, but in which we take so little interest, and with a heartless indifference so generally abandon to the wreck of time and the devastations of ignorance ... it would secure to us ... the forms and features of that simple ancient architecture, and be a typical memorial of that pure and ardent Christianity which gave it birth.

37 Hiberno-
Romanesque doorway
at Glenstal, Co.
Limerick, 1841, copied
from a medieval door
at Killaloe Cathedral.

The bitterness which shows itself in this passage would have been even greater if he could have foreseen the fate of his design. The committee decided to postpone building of the chapel and cross, and to bury O'Connell's remains in a crypt underneath the tower, against all historical precedent, and in the face of protests from Petrie and from many other people as well. The tower was built grossly out of 36 proportion, thus preventing the possibility, even if money had been available, of carrying out Petrie's design. The interior of the crypt was decorated by the firm of Early and Powells (who had taken over the Irish business of Hardman's of Birmingham), under the supervision of Daniel O'Connell, grandson of the Liberator, who had trained as an architect with J. A. Hansom.[33] The tomb, which finally received its occupant in 1869, was decorated with carvings 'in imitation of the best examples of pure Celtic ornament', taken from casts of existing work, or, ironically, from Petrie's *Irish Antiquities*. Instead of Petrie's design, which would, architecturally, have been far ahead of its time, the result was a heavily decorated and much more commonplace compendium of Celtic ornament.

Another interesting, and less abortive, instance of the revival of the Hiberno-Romanesque style is at Glenstal, Co. Limerick, a Neo-Norman castle built for Matthew Barrington in the 1830s and 1840s, chiefly by William Bardwell.[34] The doorway from the dining room to the drawing room (carved in 1841 by a local 37 man called White) is a copy of the doorway at Killaloe Cathedral, Co. Clare.

While the castle draws on various Romanesque sources, it is difficult to know why so conspicuous an Irish example has been used here, and it has been suggested that Barrington was influenced by his neighbour Lord Dunraven, of Adare, Co. Limerick, with whom he was acquainted.

It is more likely that the influence came from Lord Dunraven's son, Edwin, Viscount Adare (1812–71), who in 1850 became third Earl of Dunraven. He was a distinguished antiquarian, friend and correspondent of Petrie and Stokes, and one of the founders of the Irish Archaeological Society in 1841. His work on Irish antiquities, *Notes on Irish Architecture*, left unfinished at his death in 1871, was edited by Margaret Stokes and published in 1875. There was a history of interest in antiquities at Adare, a village very rich in medieval remains.[35] The first Earl had restored the Trinitarian abbey for use as a Roman Catholic church. It was enlarged by the third Earl, who also had a portion of the ruins 'skilfully converted into a convent for Sisters of Mercy' around 1854. His architect was P. C. Hardwick (1820–90). Adare Manor itself, remodelled from 1832 to 1876, with the assistance, among others, of Hardwick and A. W. N. Pugin (1812–52), incorporates several Irish features. The tower has Irish double-stepped battlements, and inside, in the vestibule, there are 'four round-arched doorways with jambs of polished marble, elaborately moulded and ornamented with Romanesque detail'. The house as a whole is a curious mixture of historicism and fantasy.

38

Round towers were by the middle of the century beginning to achieve the status of a national emblem. As early as 1822 Lord Brandon had erected one on his estate at Killarney.[36] They were sometimes built as belfries on churches – at the Roman Catholic churches of Slane, Co. Meath, and Leighlinbridge, Co. Carlow, for example.[37] The Protestant church at Kinneigh, Co. Cork, a plain building with round-arched openings, was built beside an existing round tower, restored to act as belfry. In the sermon preached for the consecration in 1856 this was pointed to as a symbol of continuity between the Church of Ireland and the ancient Celtic Church, 'another link in the chain of Christian Sanctuaries which have stood here as witness'.[38] Maclise's eccentric friend, Father Horgan, parish priest of Blarney, was also interested in round towers, and built one for himself – 'determined, as he said,' (wrote *The Irish Builder*) 'to puzzle posterity as antiquity had puzzled him'. W. R. LeFanu has related how this came about:[39]

39
40
41

> He was well known as an Irish scholar and antiquarian, and such was his interest in and love for the old round towers of Ireland that he determined to build a fac-simile of one in his chapel-yard as a mausoleum for himself. It is not, however, so like its prototype as he meant it to be. The difference arose in this way. A large subscription had been made in the parish for its erection, and Father Horgan rashly began to build before he had sufficiently considered whether he had enough to finish. When the tower had risen to one-half its height the funds began to fail, and as he either could not or would not raise more money in the parish, he had to cut his coat according to his cloth, and was forced to diminish its diameter. Its appearance as it stands is not unlike that of a gigantic champagne bottle.

39 The Catholic church at Leighlinbridge, Co. Carlow, with a round tower purpose-built as a belfry.

40 A medieval round tower used as belfry at Kinneigh Church, Co. Cork, consecrated in 1856.

41 *Above right:* Father Horgan's round tower at Ballygibbon, Co. Cork. The doorway at the bottom is dated 1836, the top 1845.

English architects also became interested in Irish antiquities. A. W. N. Pugin did quite a lot of work in Ireland in the 1840s, and was very influential, especially as he arrived at a time when the boom in church building was beginning.[40] He visited the Cistercian abbey at Dunbrody, Co. Wexford, and his biographer, Phoebe Stanton, has suggested that his Wexford buildings were influenced by it. In his usual incisive and forthright fashion he also pronounced on the revival of ancient Irish architecture:

> If the clergy and gentry of Ireland possessed one spark of real national feeling, they would revive and restore those solemn piles of buildings which formerly covered that island of saints, and which are associated with the holiest and most honourable recollections of her history. Many of these were indeed rude and simple; but massive and solemn, they harmonized most perfectly with the wild and rocky localities in which they were erected. The real Irish ecclesiastical architecture might be revived at a considerably less cost than is now actually expended on the construction of monstrosities; and the ignorance and apathy of the clergy on this most important subject is truly deplorable.

42 Detail of a façade in Grafton Street, Dublin, by Sir Matthew Digby Wyatt, c. 1863.

Another English architect, Sir Matthew Digby Wyatt (1820–77), who was learned in the matter of Celtic ornament, designed an interesting façade for a commercial building in Grafton Street, Dublin, an engraving of which appeared in the *Building News* in 1863. It has round-headed windows, and mouldings with geometric orna- 42 ment. The imposts have panels of interlace, more reminiscent of manuscripts than of architecture, and masks, a constantly recurring theme in Irish decoration. Except for a botched ground floor it is, miraculously, still to be seen. Another indication of the spreading knowledge of Celtic art is that it was represented in Owen Jones's *Grammar of Ornament*, published in 1856.

Among leading native architects, there were a few who manifested interest in native antiquities. This was true of Benjamin Woodward (1815–61) in his youth, though he later turned to Venetian Gothic. His partner Thomas Newenham Deane (1828–99) had a lifelong involvement with ancient Irish architecture.[41] One of his most important jobs was the rebuilding of Tuam Cathedral, Co. Galway, which was carried on in the 1860s. His scheme included the reinstatement of the old chancel 43 arch, for its original purpose, in the new cathedral. This was highly approved by 44 Petrie, with whom he corresponded on the subject. Petrie was particularly delighted to find 'that with a patriotic feeling and highly cultivated taste you have made it an essential point to preserve in all its remaining entirety, the beautiful little chancel of the ancient church'.[42] When the Church of Ireland was disestablished in 1869 a problem arose over the care of ancient monuments in its charge, and a national monuments section was set up in 1874 under the Commissioners of Public Works, with T. N. Deane as its Superintendent. Though his brief was very narrow – simply to do such repairs as would make the buildings safe, and prevent them from disintegrating further – he made very careful and sensitive surveys, and his views on restoration were enlightened.

Detail of capitals and mouldings.

43, 44 Tuam Cathedral, Co. Galway: the Romanesque chancel arch before (*above*, from the restoration appeal leaflet) and after T. N. Deane's rebuilding in the 1860s.

William Henry Lynn (1829–1915) was also involved in both restoration work
and the designing of complete buildings in a revived style. He was born in Co.
Down, but sent to school at Bannow, Co. Wexford, where he became interested
in the local medieval remains. He went into partnership with the Belfast architect
Sir Charles Lanyon (1812–89) in 1854. Two of his works of the 1860s, the restoration
and virtual rebuilding of St Doulough's, Co. Dublin (1863–64), and the design and
building of St Patrick's Church, Jordanstown, Co. Antrim (1865–68), are important 45
examples of the revival of an Irish medieval style.[43] Since St Doulough's was
technically a restoration, St Patrick's could be described as 'The First Attempt in
Modern Times to Revive the Ancient Architecture of Ireland' – and, indeed, it
was much more consistent than anything that had been done so far. In general style
the building was described as 'of the tenth century'. It is fairly plain, with round-
headed openings and rough cut stone. The belfry is in the form of a round tower,
adapted in form and position from the one on Teampul Finghin at Clonmacnoise.
It gives the church an Irish appearance, though this is contradicted by the rounded
apse – a feature which only occurs in one early building, Mellifont Abbey, and
that had not been excavated in 1865.[44] Stained glass for the church was made by
Clayton and Bell of London, and since there were no tenth-century models the
details were carefully adapted from other sources. Windows in the chancel represent

46 Stained glass in St Patrick's, Jordanstown, by Clayton and Bell, showing St Patrick as bishop.

St Patrick, St Brigid, St Columba, and St Comgall, a native of Co. Antrim. The booklet published for the inauguration of the church tells us that these men flourished at a most remarkable time in Irish ecclesiastical history, when, significantly, 'the Church of Ireland formed . . . no integral part of the Church of Rome'. The three men are shown with the Irish tonsure, from ear to ear across the head, and the costumes were carefully adapted from monuments and illuminations: St Patrick's crozier, for example, was copied from one in the British Museum.

Finally, among leading Catholic architects, we have J. J. McCarthy (1817–82), 'the Irish Pugin'.[45] He was a close friend of Gavan Duffy, to the extent of being on the organizing committee of a banquet which was given for Duffy before he went into political exile in 1855, though by this he risked antagonizing Archbishop Cullen, who did not approve of political agitators, and on whom a Catholic architect would be dependent for commissions. McCarthy was a companion of the men of Young Ireland, probably also belonged to the Repeal Association, and he read *The Nation*. He later told Duffy that it was from this that he had 'caught the first impulse to revive the Irish Gothic in ecclesiastical buildings'.[46] The mention of Gothic is significant: McCarthy was not, on the whole, a reviver of Irish Romanesque, but he did look for inspiration to Irish Gothic, though with some reservations:[47]

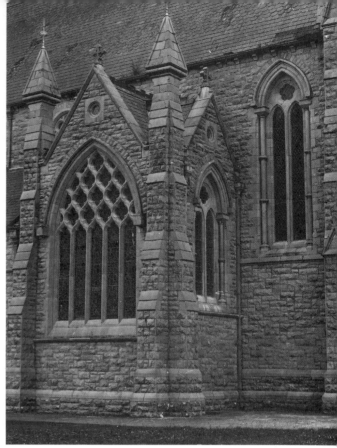

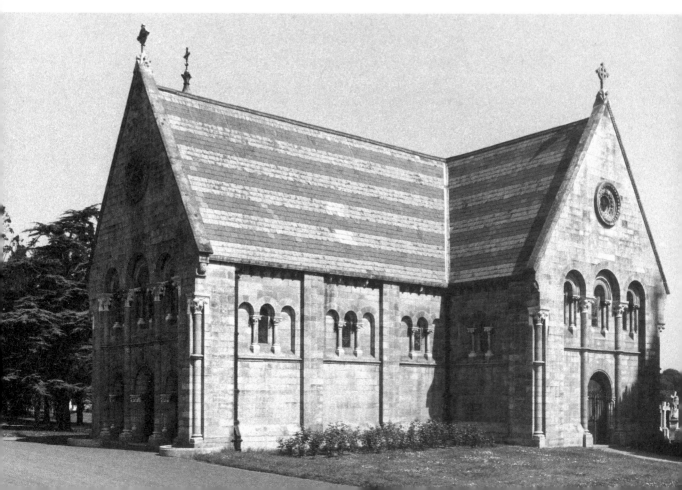

we hope our nationality will not carry us beyond the bounds of strict truth; and we therefore do not claim for our country that which manifestly she never possessed, those grand developments of ecclesiastical art which have been the pride and the shame of other countries.

He also felt that designers should look as much as possible at foreign sources until more was known about Irish architecture. At St Brendan, Ardfert, Co. Kerry (1851–53), he modelled his tracery on a window in the transept of the ancient cathedral, and for SS. Peter and Paul at Kilmallock, Co. Limerick (1878), he drew on details 48 from the neighbouring Dominican friary, especially for the window of the Lady 47 Chapel. From Romanesque architecture he occasionally used the round tower, though not in an authentic manner. At Lixnaw, Co. Kerry (1861), it serves as a bellcote, high on the west front of the church, and at Thomastown, Co. Kilkenny (1858), the staircase turrets are circular, but are engaged and look more German or French than Irish. Only in the Mortuary Chapel at Glasnevin (completed in 1878) 49 does McCarthy try to be wholeheartedly Hiberno-Romanesque. He uses chevron and billet mouldings 'modelled on Irish Romanesque examples', and the gallery over the west porch is reached by means of a round tower 'of the ancient Irish type', also used as a belfry.[48] The reason for the choice of style was that the chapel was intended to complement the O'Connell round tower, and thus complete 36 Petric's group. McCarthy, however, like so many revivers of Hiberno-Romanesque, could not resist a cruciform plan and semicircular apse, neither a feature of the Irish style.

The Catholic and Protestant Churches vied with each other to build churches based on ancient models (not necessarily Irish) in an effort to establish continuity with the early Church. Both communions were interested in the liturgy of medieval times, a fact attested by the societies established for the study of ecclesiology – the Down, Connor and Dromore Church Architecture Society, founded in 1842 (Church of Ireland); the Irish Ecclesiological Society, founded in 1849 (Roman Catholic); and St Patrick's Society for the Study of Ecclesiology, founded in 1855 (Church of Ireland). There is an interesting sidelight on the rivalry in the booklet published for the inauguration of the Protestant St Patrick's, Jordanstown. It in- 45 cludes notes on the life of St Patrick, which claim that 'The confusion of facts and dates which causes so much perplexity in the history of St Patrick is due in a great measure to the continuous attempts of Roman Catholic writers to connect his mission with the See of Rome.'[49] It seems likely that for Roman Catholics the Gothic Revival as a whole was a sign of revived strength, and a return to a hazily perceived period when Ireland was free, Catholic (Protestantism was, after all, an English import), and an international focus for saints and scholars. Politics and religion were inextricably mixed, a fact attested by the *Irish Catholic Directory* of 1845:[50]

We hope yet to see the day when the zealous piety of the people, guided by educated taste, will once more cover the face of the 'Island of Saints' with structures that shall emulate the sacred splendour of the august fanes which were the boast of 'Cashel of 103 the Kings' or of holy Mellifont, and whose ruins remain to attest the ruthless atrocity of our Saxon invaders.

47, 48 The Lady Chapel of J. J. McCarthy's church of SS. Peter and Paul at Kilmallock, Co. Limerick, 1878, and its model in the medieval friary nearby.

49 J. J. McCarthy: Mortuary Chapel in Glasnevin Cemetery, Dublin, designed in the early 1870s and completed in 1878.

CHAPTER 5

Popular and applied arts

IT WAS IN THE APPLIED ARTS, rather than in the more sober fine arts, that popular Irish symbolism was used in the most exuberant fashion. Stonecarvers, stuccodores, makers of furniture and souvenirs in bog oak, jewellers producing reproductions of Celtic ornaments, were much less inhibited than their brethren in the Academies, and there was an upsurge of national sentiment which lasted until the end of the century. It was not national feeling, however, as it was to be understood among the patriots and intellectuals of the early twentieth century. Shamrocks are often found in association with the rose and the thistle, or with oak leaves, both combina- 64 tions being emblematic of the Union of Great Britain and Ireland. Loyalty, even 65 servility, to the Crown was the usual thing, at least among the tradesmen in the souvenir business. Waterhouse of Dublin was especially proud of the fact that Queen Victoria bought two copies of the brooch he called the Royal Tara Brooch. Arthur 11 Jones, the Dublin cabinetmaker, included in his suite of furniture illustrative of Irish history a statuette of the Queen with a wolfhound looking up at her 'with 66 attachment', his paws on a heart-shaped shield bearing the words *Cuisle mo croidhe* which can be loosely translated as 'the darling of my heart'.

Ornamental stonecarving in Ireland, as elsewhere in Europe, received great impetus in the nineteenth century. This was due to the medieval revivals, and to the growing taste for styles of architecture which required elaborate ornament. Most of it was of a conventional kind – animals and foliage, heads as corbels and label-stops, standard medieval motifs like stiff leaf, ballflower, chevron and dog-tooth – but there was a great deal that was original and exciting. This was partly due to the influence of Ruskin, which induced Benjamin Woodward in the Museum for Trinity College and in the Kildare Street Club, both in Dublin, to give his carvers 51 a free hand, a procedure which brought talents like the O'Shea brothers into the open. They also worked for Woodward at Oxford, where their carvings included the famous 'parrots and owls' on the University Museum, and their nephew Whelan worked for Waterhouse on the Manchester Assize Courts. The traffic was not just one-way: English carvers came as journeymen to Ireland, and some stayed and established themselves in business. C. W. Harrison, who is credited with the billiard- 99 playing monkeys on the Kildare Street Club, came from Yorkshire about 1859.[1] 101 James Pearse, father of Patrick and Willie, came from Birmingham, and was a jour-neyman with Harrison, who had by then set up in business on his own account.[2]

By the middle of the century Irish motifs and symbolism had become fairly perva-sive, so it was natural that they should creep in among more conventional work. In addition to this, it was fashionable to give carvers a certain amount of freedom,

50 O'Meara's Irish House, Dublin, decorated by Burnet and Comerford in 1870. See p. 76.

51 Shamrock on a subsidiary entrance to Deane and Woodward's Kildare Street Club, Dublin, 1858–61, possibly carved by one of the O'Shea brothers.

52 Daniel O'Connell wearing the 'Milesian crown': label stop of the west door of St James's, Dublin, by Patrick Byrne, 1844–59.

53 Harp and shamrock at the west end of the nave of St Patrick's Cathedral, Armagh, completed by J. J. McCarthy in 1853–73.

and to allow them to please themselves about what they carved, within the limits of an architectural scheme. The subsidiary entrance to the Kildare Street Club has 51 a trailing spray of shamrock-like foliage round the door. At the church of St James in Dublin, begun in 1844, the label stops on the west doorway are portraits of Father Canavan, the parish priest, and Daniel O'Connell wearing the 'Milesian 52 crown' (see p. 38). The Catholic church at Kilcock, Co. Kildare, designed by J. J. McCarthy, has an altar dated 1862 of which the reredos is surrounded by a decorative panel of what looks at first sight like a Gothic diaper pattern: on closer 2 inspection, however, this proves to be made up of wolfhounds, shamrocks, harps and round towers, only the last of which has any religious significance whatsoever. It is another instance of the identification of nationalism and religion. There is also an example at St Patrick's Roman Catholic Cathedral, Armagh, where there is a little carved group of harp and shamrock at the springing of one of the arches in 53 the nave arcade. The Catholic church at Clara, Co. Offaly, designed possibly in the 1870s by J. J. O'Callaghan,[3] has shamrocks both inside and out – inside for an entire capital and as a label stop, and outside on the tympanum of the west door, where an angel bears a shield with harp and shamrock on it. In addition to this kind of popular ornament, the churches which represent a deliberate revival of ancient Irish styles have carving which is native in a more antiquarian way.

Another vigorous branch of the stonecarving business was in gravestones and funerary monuments. This overlapped with architectural carving, in the case of Harrison, for example, and even with 'fine art' sculptors, in the case of prolific Dublin families like the Farrells and the Kirks. Gravestones and monuments often take a popularly patriotic turn with harps, shamrocks and wolfhounds. In addition, monuments adapted or copied from the ancient high crosses became, after the middle of the century, very common indeed, and Henry O'Neill's book on Irish sculptured crosses, published in 1857, was a very useful source of models. This seems 8 to have become quite an industry: by the end of the century the export of crosses to England, and to America and Canada, was substantial.

High crosses abound in the Dublin Catholic cemetery at Glasnevin – plain crosses, crosses with interlace ornament, crosses with carved scenes. They are also to be found in the other major Dublin graveyard, Mount Jerome, though less profusely: it is older, and predominantly Protestant. The most striking of the crosses at Glas- nevin are around the O'Connell round tower – aptly enough, since Petrie's scheme 36 included a cross. One of the most picturesque is the monument to Ellen Burke, 57 who died in 1879, and her husband William, who died in 1885. It was designed by the architect W. H. Byrne (1844–1917), and sculptured by the firm of Pearse and Sharp (James Pearse took into partnership his foreman Edmund Sharp, who had also come to Ireland as a journeyman carver). On three sides of its base the cross has scenes from the life of St Patrick: they show him during his first visit to Ireland, minding sheep (also a pig and a cow), with shamrock at his feet, and, improbably, a round tower on a distant hillside; baptizing the King of Munster 58 – a scene which includes a sunburst, round tower, and a rather diminutive wolf- hound; and holding a shamrock leaf almost as big as his head, expounding the Trinity. Even less sophisticated is the monument to John Keegan Casey (1846–70),

54 Celtic crosses in the college graveyard at Maynooth, Co. Kildare, burial place of many Irish bishops in the 19th century.

55 Detail of the cross to the 18th-century priest and patriot Father Sheehy at Clogheen, Co. Tipperary, by Lonergan of Clonmel, 1870.

56 Base of the monument to John Keegan Casey in Glasnevin Cemetery, Dublin, 1870.

author of the patriotic song *The Rising of the Moon*, which has, around its base, harp, shamrock, round tower, Celtic cross, and a very shaggy wolfhound. In front 56 of the Catholic church at Clogheen, Co. Tipperary, is a cross in memory of Father Nicholas Sheehy, parish priest of Clogheen, erected in 1870, carved by a local man, 55 Lonergan of Clonmel. It is an extraordinary mixture of religious and patriotic symbolism: at the top is the sun and then a shamrock, then the Crucifixion, flanked by winged angels with chalices; lower down are Daniel O'Connell, Erin asleep, watched, apparently, by St Patrick, and much else. The cross is entirely covered in such little vignettes. Not all crosses have narrative scenes on them: some just have panels of abstract ornament, spirals, interlace, grotesque animals. Some of it is of 1 very high quality, and some commonplace. In Mount Jerome Cemetery there is a curious monument to James Haughton, who died in 1873. A mixture of anti- 59 quarian and popular ornament, it is in the form of a Hiberno-Romanesque door-way, and at its base it has sprays of shamrock climbing up, very finely carved.

74

57, 58 *Left and bottom:* high cross of Ellen and William Burke (d. 1879 and 1885) in Glasnevin Cemetery, Dublin. The detail of the sculpture, by Pearse and Sharp, shows St Patrick baptizing the King of Munster (see p. 36).

59 *Below:* monument of James Haughton in Mount Jerome Cemetery, Dublin, 1873.

Coats of arms, emblems, and trophy groups were another area where national
sentiment could manifest itself. With Daniel O'Connell among its founders, the
National Bank had particularly patriotic connections. Its head office, in College
Green, Dublin, remodelled in 1889 to the design of Charles Geoghegan (1820–1908),
was crowned with a group by Pearse and Sharp.[4] It shows Erin with her harp (which 60
has interlace decoration), a wolfhound at her feet, and the ancient Irish crown by
her side; various emblems of trade and commerce are 'disposed around her in a
suitable manner', and her pedestal is inscribed *Éire go Bragh* (Ireland for ever).

More popular still in its imagery was decoration executed in plaster or Portland
cement, especially on shops and public houses. The most spectacular of all was done
by Burnet and Comerford of Dublin in 1870, on O'Meara's Irish House on Wood 50
Quay, Dublin.[5] The façade was divided up by pilasters with niches containing wolfhounds and methers (ancient Irish drinking cups, appropriate on a pub). Between
the pilasters were Irish patriotic scenes – Daniel O'Connell, clearly in full enjoyment
of his oratorical power, Erin weeping over her stringless harp, Grattan's Last Address
to the Irish Parliament, an illustration of Tom Moore's song *Rich and Rare*. Above
these, silhouetted against the sky, was a crown of six very tall round towers, linked
at their base with decorative ironwork incorporating the date and the mottoes *Erin
go Bragh and Céad Míle Fáilte*. This building has, inexcusably, been demolished.
Less spectacular, but still extant, is the pediment ornament of a pub in Ringsend, 61
Dublin, which has the familiar group of round tower, cross and wolfhound. In
the same vein, and spread liberally over the façades of Listowel, Co. Kerry, is the
work of Pat McAuliffe (1846–1921).[6] He began as a builder, and, becoming interested in relief decoration, embellished houses in the town with ornamented
groups. The Harp and Lion Bar has a harp and a lion, Celtic interlace beasts holding 62
shamrocks in their beaks, and inscriptions in three languages: *Erin go Bragh, Maison
de Ville*, and *Spes Mea in Deo*. Even more spectacular is the Central Hotel, with 1
a bosomy Erin leaning on her harp, a round tower beside her, and a wolfhound at
her feet. The inscription, wreathed in interlace and shamrock, is *Erin go Bragh*.

The manufacture of furniture was another area in which characteristically Irish themes and symbols were used, especially as quite a lot of furniture, made from native woods, was intended for sale to tourists as souvenirs. Bog wood, that is wood dug up from turf bogs, where it had seasoned and gained rich colour, was very common, and in districts where there was no new timber it was used for gates and gateposts, fences and hurdles, and as supports for grain stacks. It was also burnt as firewood. Its use for decorative inlay in furniture goes back at least to the seventeenth century, but it gained great popularity in the nineteenth. Killarney, being very rich in natural timber as well as bog wood, and the most important tourist centre, especially after the railway reached it in 1854, had a thriving furniture industry, mostly inlaid pieces known as Killarney work. It is discussed in *Slater's Directory to Killarney and Neighbourhood*, published in 1856:[7]

> An important branch of business is established here, in the manufacture of fancy articles similar to the Tunbridge ware goods; they are formed from the wood of the beautiful arbutus tree that flourishes in the islands of and mountains surrounding the lakes and is not to be met with elsewhere in such perfection and maturity as in this romantic region.

As late as 1892, the *Souvenir of the Lakes of Killarney and Glengarrif* encourages the visitor to visit the 'Arbutus Factories', where every species of useful article is made out of arbutus and other woods of the district. Young damsels, carrying basketfuls of the smaller articles (needle cases, paper cutters, card cases) assailed strangers in the street. Jeremiah O'Connor, 'Arbutus and Bog Oak Manufacturer', Main Street, Killarney, was a leading furniture maker. He is mentioned in the guide of 1856, and sent to the Royal Dublin Society Exhibition of 1861 'tables, work-boxes, chess-

63 Arthur Jones of Dublin: davenport inlaid with coloured wood, known as Killarney work (coll. Mr Geoffrey O'Connor). At the top is Glena Cottage.

64 Arthur Jones of
Dublin: detail of a table
of Killarney work,
showing Muckross
Friary and Glena
Cottage (Muckross
House, Killarney). The
decoration includes
shamrock, thistle and
rose.
65 Box of Killarney
work, showing
Muckross Friary, Glena
Cottage, and perhaps
Ross Castle. Note the
varied shading of the
designs repeated on the
sides and top of the
box, and their
resemblance to the
Jones furniture inlay
(ills. 63, 64), suggesting
common models.

boards, and ornaments made from the different woods peculiar to Killarney; views of Killarney on arbutus wood, inlaid with laburnum'. He was still in operation in 1882, when he sent inlaid arbutus and carved bog oak to the Dublin Exhibition. The Ulster Museum has a davenport veneered with yew and inlaid with various coloured woods which was probably made by him: the inlaid scenes, in oval frames, represent local antiquities – Muckross Friary, Ross Castle, Aghadoe, Inisfallen, and also, on the lid, Glena Cottage, where Queen Victoria had luncheon when she visited Killarney in 1861.[8] J. Egan of Main Street, Killarney, was another manufacturer who specialized in 'fancy furniture in arbutus wood, inlaid', specimens of which he sent to the Dublin Exhibitions of 1853 and 1865.[9] Not all such furniture was made in Killarney: the Dublin firm of Arthur J. Jones, Son & Co. also produced a davenport of inlaid bog yew. Pieces of this kind seem to have been fairly common, and even more so were work-boxes with the same kind of scenes. So similar are many of the inlaid pictures that it seems not improbable that they were manufactured in bulk and sold to different cabinetmakers; and even when the inlay treatment varies, the drawing often shows a common prototype.

63
64
65

1 Erin, by Pat McAuliffe, on the façade of the Central Hotel at Listowel, Co. Kerry. See p. 76.

A great deal of ornamental Irish furniture was shown at the Great Exhibition in London in 1851,[10] and at the Irish exhibitions it inspired – Cork in 1852, Dublin in 1853, 1865, and so on. Being heavily decorated, and often including a narrative element, it appealed to contemporary taste, though the official report on the Dublin Exhibition of 1853 did venture to criticize furniture of 'extravagant ornamentation without much regard to appropriateness of design'.[11] This criticism is certainly applicable to Arthur Jones, who exhibited a suite of furniture in Irish bog yew in London in 1851 and Dublin in 1853, and a selection at the Royal Dublin Society's show of 1861. He published an illustrated pamphlet, *Description of a Suite of Sculptured Decorative Furniture*, to publicize his wares in 1853.[12] The bog yew, he said, resembled the subject it illustrated, Irish history and antiquities:

> As the details of Irish history have been disentombed from the oblivion which conquest entails upon the records of the vanquished, the bog yew timber of ancient Ireland has been exhumed from the depths of her peat formations; and it must be observed that the material possesses an aesthetic virtue besides the appropriateness of this association.

The wood also conveyed the idea of antiquity by its tints. The suite consisted of a cabriolet sofa, an occasional table, a circular table, a teapoy, an omnium or what-not, a whist table, a stand for a timepiece, a pair of pole firescreens, an armchair, a semicircular side table, a sarcophagus or wine-cooler and a 'music temple'. The sofa had pillows in the form of shamrocks. The teapoy was designed to represent the ancient commerce of Ireland, with a figure of Commerce on the summit, and a bas relief on the front representing Hibernia inviting commerce, in the form of a Tyrian merchant galley, to the shores of Ireland. She was shown seated beneath the basalt cliffs of the Giant's Causeway, on the heights of which could be seen a giant elk. The base of the teapoy showed the giant elk, pursued by wolfhounds, entangled in an oak forest. The armchair had arms in the form of wolfhounds, one at ease, recumbent, with the motto on his collar 'Gentle when stroked', the other erect and angry, with the motto 'Fierce when provoked'. Most spectacular of all

67
68

66, 67 Arthur Jones of Dublin: woodwork illustrated in 1853. *Left*, a statuette of Queen Victoria, seated on a throne made of the horns of extinct Irish elks (see p. 71). *Right*, an armchair of bog yew shown at the Crystal Palace in 1851.

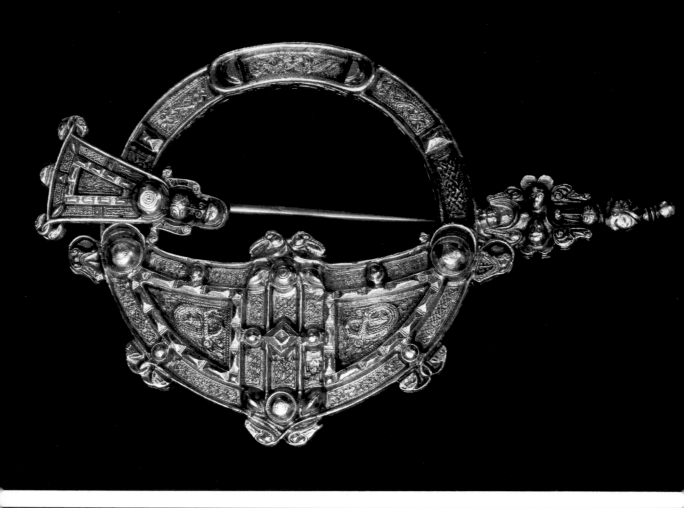
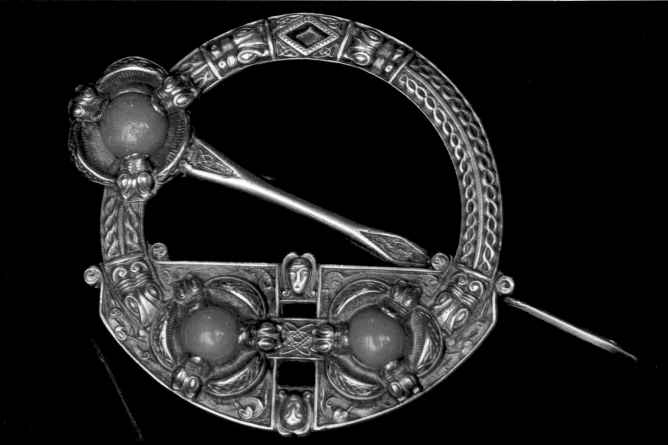

was the music temple. On its summit sat Ollamh Fodhla, seated on the *lia fáil*, or 68
Stone of Destiny, 'now reputed to be deposited in Westminster Abbey' (that is,
the Coronation Stone), on a platform representing all Ireland mapped out under
him, the coastline 'exhibiting prominent scenery of the four provinces'. The four
panels on the sides of the piece showed (on the long sides) the opening of the Tri-
ennial Convention at Tara and the harpers in Tara's Hall performing before the
monarch and his queen, and (on the ends) portraits of Onaoi, 'the first musician
who accompanied the sons of Milesius to Ireland', and Carolan, 'who may be
regarded as the last of the Irish bards'. The lower stretcher had the initials V and
A 'embosomed' in the heart of a bunch of shamrocks, the date, 1851, and 'Erin'
inscribed in ornamental capitals from the Book of Kells.

II Waterhouse and
Co.: 'Royal Tara
Brooch', a parcel gilt
copy made in the 1850s
of the famous brooch
that belonged to
Waterhouse (Ulster
Museum, Belfast). See
ill. 9 and p. 87.

III Parcel gilt copy of
the Cavan Brooch, set
with coral bosses
(Ulster Museum,
Belfast), probably made
after 1852: other
jewellers were quick to
follow Waterhouse's
lead. Like the 'Royal
Tara Brooch' in ill. II, it
is 7 cm. (2¾ in.) in
diameter.

68 Arthur Jones of
Dublin: 'music temple'
shown at the Crystal
Palace in 1851.

J. Kerr of Stafford Street, Dublin, made an oak chair for the Council Chamber of the Corporation of Dublin, with arms supported by wolfhounds and the Civic Arms on the back. It was shown at the Dublin Exhibition of 1853. Patrick Beakey was another manufacturer with a huge warehouse in Stafford Street. In 1853 he seems to have been in partnership with a man called McDowell: they sent to the Dublin Exhibition of that year a sideboard with figures on it of Peace, Plenty, Sculpture, Architecture, England and Ireland. Beakey alone exhibited furniture in the Gothic style at the exhibition of 1865. He also made at least two pieces for Daniel O'Connell, a table and a chair.[13] The table, dating from 1861, is of oak, with a pedestal in the form of a round tower, almost hidden by branches of oak and harps, 69 and a recumbent wolfhound on each of the three feet. The chair, which was carved by Gaussen, has an elaborate back, with harp, round towers and wolfhounds. The dog-collars and harp strings are of Wicklow gold. A fourth Dublin furniture maker, C. Clarke of Stephen's Green, sent to the 1853 exhibition a 'davenport, on richly carved consoles, with guard on top representing the round towers of Ireland'.

Belfast also had furniture makers working in the same vein. In 1865 H. McCormick, of that city, won an award for his bog oak work. The Ulster Museum has a bog oak chair by Dawson Bell of Belfast. It has a richly carved back, which shows a harp surmounted by a shield with the Red Hand of Ulster, and flanked by shamrock and wolfhound. Above this central group is a cap-like object, an illustration of which appeared in the *Dublin Penny Journal* of 25 August 1832, where it was described as an ancient Irish crown, made of gold, discovered in Co. Tipperary in 1692. The chair back also incorporates oak leaves and acorns, which in this context symbolize the Union.

An activity which was allied to the manufacture of furniture, but often separate from it, was the souvenir trade in jewellery and small objects carved out of bog wood, usually oak. According to an article in the *Illustrated Catalogue* to the Dublin Exhibition of 1865, this began with the visit of George IV to Ireland in 1821, when a man called M'Gurk carved a walking stick of bog oak and presented it to the King. It was admired, and M'Gurk got orders for more. Some time later a Killarney man called Connell (perhaps the Denis Connell who showed 'a great variety of bog oak ornaments' in Cork in 1852[14]) began to carve oak from the bogs near the town, and sell it to tourists as souvenirs. He did very well, and moved to Dublin some time in the 1840s. *The Art Journal* in 1865 traced the popularity of the material to a certain John Neate, who 'so far back as 1820 manufactured articles from bog wood, and was certainly among the first to profess it, if he did not actually originate the trade'.[15] His business was inherited by his son-in-law, Cornelius Goggin. The Goggin family figure largely in the trade: in 1861 there were Goggin and Cremmin of Killarney and Nassau Street, Dublin, C. Goggin of Nassau Street, and J. Goggin of Grafton Street, Dublin.[16] The *Art Journal* article also spoke of three ladies called Grierson, 'persons of education and refinement', who lived in the Dublin mountains, and taught wood carving, as they had seen it practised in Sweden, to local people. They had several pupils who made bog wood souvenirs, including a man named Thomas Rogers who was particularly good. He would come down into Dublin from Glenasmole, collect his orders and wood and retire to his valley again. He carved, for Johnson of Suffolk Street, the bog oak box made to hold the Irish lace presented to the Princess of Wales by the ladies of Ireland, 'one of the most elaborate and beautiful pieces of work that has ever been produced'. Whoever was responsible for starting the bog oak industry, there can be no doubt of its success. By the time of the great exhibitions from 1851 onwards it was flourishing, and largely represented. Even before that, Mrs Asenath Nicholson of New York, who toured Ireland in 1844–45, and visited 'the annual exhibition of the arts' (probably, since it included furniture, at the Royal Dublin Society), admired the bog oak, which, she said, was a specimen of the wealth of this neglected island 'in its bowels as well as upon its surface'.[17] She saw tables, chairs, and small fancy articles of the most exquisite beauty, and a sculptured group entitled *Father Mathew Administering the Pledge to a Peasant*, said to be – though this is difficult to believe – 'as large as life'. By 1865 one Dublin firm alone, Johnson, was selling £4,000 or £5,000 worth a year, and other leading manufacturers, like Goggin, were doing just as well. Shops selling such souvenirs must have been common enough for Sir William Wilde's mistress to be described simply as 'a woman who kept a black oak shop'.[18] Johnson invented a method of mass production, stamping patterns by placing the bog oak on a die and subjecting it to heat and pressure. The bitumen in it prevented it from cracking. The results are fairly detailed, but not as sharp as carving. Bog oak was even faked. 'It is to be regretted', wrote *The Art Journal* in 1865, 'that a very inferior imitation is produced in England, made of common deal, stamped and coloured, which is sold as genuine Irish carved bog oak. It can, however, deceive only the very ignorant or the very unwary.'

Articles in bog oak are on the whole small, ranging from brooches a few centimetres wide to wine-coolers, caskets, and 'a multitude of objects used in the boudoir

69 Beakey of Dublin: base of an oak table made in 1861 for Daniel O'Connell (Derrynane Abbey, Co. Kerry).

and the drawing room'.[19] The workmanship is sometimes very fine and delicate, but more usually coarse and awkward, clear evidence of an unsophisticated folk art. The catalogue of the Dublin Exhibition of 1853 attributed this to 'the rudeness of design and coarseness of execution naturally inseparable from the infancy of the trade',[20] but the standard did not necessarily improve with time. Sometimes the oak was embellished with other materials. Acheson of Dublin exhibited in 1853 a casket of 'black bog oak ... enriched with silver gilt mountings and national emblems, the jewels being Irish diamonds [iron pyrites] and amethysts which have a peculiarly brilliant effect when mounted on the dark bog wood'. To the same exhibition West and Son of College Green sent a casket 'after the Irish antique, of bog yew, Cork malachite, and natural gold and silver studded with Irish pearls, amethysts, carbuncles etc.' The Ulster Museum (whose Hull Grundy Collection contains the finest assemblage of bog oak and metal jewellery) has a brooch of bog oak which shows Erin sitting on a bank, playing her harp. The bank is studded 71 with little gold shamrocks, and the harp-strings are also made of gold.

The motifs used in bog oak carving were generally Irish, but ran the full gamut from popular to antiquarian. Brooches were made in imitation of the 'Tara' Brooch, or showed Irish architectural antiquities, for example the castles of Dangan, Crom and Malahide, and the abbeys of Holy Cross and Dunbrody. Scenes round Killarney 72 were popular for sale to tourists as souvenirs. A brooch in the Ulster Museum shows Muckross Friary in a wreath of ferns. Ferns were a Victorian craze, not particularly Irish, except that they are plentiful round Killarney, where even rare varieties were found and avidly collected, and where they were often used in carved and inlaid decoration.

Tara Pin

Bracelets of bog oak were also popular. Acheson of Dublin made 'elastic band bracelets, with fibulae and bog oak mountings'. Goggin of Nassau Street, Dublin, sent to the Dublin Exhibition of 1853 'bracelets, brooches, necklaces, earrings, studs, buttons, card-cases, bookstands, chessboards and other articles of jewellery in bog oak, Killarney arbutus and yew, [and] connemara marble'. One of the Goggin firms made necklaces and bracelets of 'Irish diamonds' set in silver, in the shape of chains 75 of shamrocks. Ornaments were also made to stand on mantelpieces and whatnots: 80 there were models of high crosses, round towers, castles and abbeys, and sometimes groups of antiquities like Glendalough or Muckross. The poet Thomas Moore owned a harp of bog oak, now in the National Museum of Ireland, which is about 15 centimetres (6 inches) high, and very finely carved with a garland of shamrocks.

At the lowest end of the iconographic scale there were comic 'Irish' scenes, reminiscent of the ape-like depictions of Irishmen so dear to *Punch*. These included such subjects as 'Donnybrook Fair' (notorious for fights), 'The Tail of my Coat', and 'Paddy and his Pig', 'in which the pig, proverbial for going the contrary way to that which it is wanted to go, is deceived with a knowing leer by Paddy, who pretends that he is going the wrong way, and thereby induces his pig to go right'. This last, by Mr Samuels of Nassau Street, was praised in the catalogue of the Dublin Exhibition of 1865.

The area of popular and applied art in which antiquarian studies had the most profound and striking effect was in the making of jewellery. Ancient Celtic ornaments, collected and made known by bodies like the Royal Irish Academy, caught the eye of the Dublin jewellers, who began to make copies and imitations. Most

70 Waterhouse and Co.: three illustrations from *Ornamental Irish Antiquities*, 1852.

prominent among these was the firm of Waterhouse and Co., who publicized their wares with great vigour, notably in the pamphlet *Ornamental Irish Antiquities*, published in 1852 and reprinted in 1853. For several years past, they said, the only ornaments of a national character to be had were made from bog oak, 'both inelegant in design and rudely finished'. Then, in 1842, at the suggestion of Corry Connellan of Dublin Castle, they converted a copy of an antique fibula, by the addition of a joint and pin, into a brooch. In 1849 the Royal Irish Academy allowed them to make drawings and copies of antique brooches in its collection, which led to an extensive manufacture. By 1853 their range included the Clarendon Brooch, the Royal Tara Brooch, the Knights Templar Brooch, the Dublin University Brooch, the Innisfallen Brooch, and many others. One of the earliest to be copied was the Ballyspellan Brooch (in the possession of the Royal Dublin Society), which has an Ogham inscription on the back. Waterhouse called one version the Ogham Pin and another the Clarendon Shawl Brooch, after the Countess of Clarendon, the Viceroy's wife, who first patronized it. They manufactured it in silver, in gold with Irish pearls, and in silver gilt inlaid with bog oak, 'Irish diamonds', Irish malachite, and Irish amethysts, and by 1853 had sold more than two thousand, at prices between one pound and eight guineas. The discovery of the so-called 'Tara' Brooch in 1850 gave added impetus to the fashion, since it is the most elaborate and beautiful of all. It was picked up, according to a contemporary account which may or may not be true, on the seashore by the children of a poor woman, who sold it to a watchmaker in the nearby town of Drogheda.[21] He in turn sold it to Waterhouse. Petrie read a paper on it to the Royal Irish Academy in December 1850, and Waterhouse was eventually persuaded (though not till 1868) to part with it to the Academy. Petrie had ended his paper with the words:[22]

> I cannot but feel assured that Mr Waterhouse, who has derived a great pecuniary benefit from our exertions to create an interest in such remains, will feel it is due to us in return to give a deaf ear to all temptations to seduce him to let this Brooch out of Ireland, and that he will have a pleasure as well as feel it his interest, to see it placed in its proper depository.

It was presumably Waterhouse who named it the 'Tara Brooch', a name sufficiently evocative and romantic to catch the popular imagination. The brooch was not found at, or even particularly near, Tara, but the name has stuck, and resisted all attempts to get rid of it. It was known as the 'Royal Tara Brooch' after Waterhouse had had the honour of showing it to Queen Victoria and Prince Albert at Windsor in 1850: the Queen bought two copies, and imitations and adaptations became very popular. It is indeed the best known of all the brooches, so that the others tend to be known, generically, as Tara Brooches. Waterhouse made a companion piece, the Tara Bracelet, adapting motifs from the brooch. He also produced brooches of a different kind, adapted from the shape of the ancient Irish harp, notably the one known as Brian Boru's Harp in Trinity College, Dublin.

Several manufacturers followed his lead. West and Son of College Green registered patterns for Celtic brooches in 1849, and had a large exhibit at the Crystal Palace in 1851. There were extensive displays at the Dublin Exhibitions of 1853 and 1865, by which time, as Waterhouse put it, Ireland could boast of 'the continued use of peculiarly national ornaments worn by her princes and nobles in ages long since past'.[23]

Innisfallen Brooch

Brian Borhrome's Harp

71, 72 Brooches of bog oak, *c.* 1850 (Ulster Museum, Belfast). One shows Erin with a gilt-stringed harp, seated on a mound sprinkled with gold shamrocks; the other shows Malahide Castle, in an unusual border based perhaps on the carving of high crosses.

73, 74 Waterhouse and Co.: front and back of a silver-gilt copy of the Ballyspellan Brooch, known as the 'Ogham Pin' or 'Clarendon Brooch', registered in 1849 (Ulster Museum, Belfast).

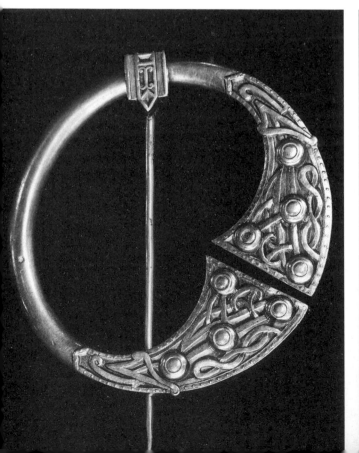
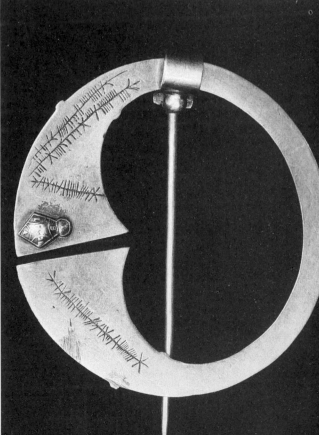

75 Bracelet of 'Irish diamonds', or iron pyrites, set in silver in the style of Goggin of Dublin, *c.* 1850 (Ulster Museum, Belfast).

76 Waterhouse and Co.: 'Tara Bracelet', of silver gilt, probably designed *c.* 1851 (Ulster Museum, Belfast). It was intended to complement the 'Royal Tara Brooches' made by the firm (ill. 11), and was like them based on the ancient brooch (ill. 9).

77, 78 Round towers, harps, wolfhounds and shamrock on velvet and on glass: livery of a coachman of the Lord Mayor of Dublin, 1888–89 (Civic Museum, Dublin), and detail of a jug by Pugh of Dublin, 1880s (coll. Mrs Mary Boydell).

By the third quarter of the nineteenth century 'Irishry', generally of a popular kind, had spread to many of the applied arts, and it continued to flourish. A Lord Mayor of Dublin in the 1880s dressed his coach servants in green livery, with 77 embroidered decoration of round towers, wolfhounds, and shamrocks. When electric street lighting came to Dublin in 1892 the cast-iron lamp standards, though 79 manufactured in England, were decorated with shamrocks.[24] They were very pretty, even elegant, and many still survive. Dublin glass-houses, like the firm of Pugh in the 1880s, produced tableware – jugs, glasses, and goblets – ornamented with exuberant sprays of shamrock which accord very well with the full shapes of the vessels they decorate.[25] More elaborate ornaments are to be found, including the inevitable group of round tower, wolfhound and harp, and sentiments like *Erin* 78 *go Bragh*. Some of this very fine engraving was done by Bohemian glass workers in Dublin.

National sentiment expressed itself in pottery and porcelain, particularly that produced at Belleek, Co. Fermanagh.[26] The factory was founded in the late 1850s or early 1860s, and its familiar emblem of round tower, harp, hound and shamrock was used from early in its history. The factory had a staple production of ordinary pottery and stoneware for domestic use, but quite early on began to experiment with porcelain. Typical examples are exceedingly thin, with a creamy, nacreous glaze, and fine naturalistic detail. By the end of the 1860s Belleek was well known for the high artistic quality of its porcelain, produced for a luxury market. As with other such products, the seal was set on its fashion by orders from Queen Victoria, the Prince of Wales, and members of the nobility. The founders of the factory brought in skilled workers from the firm of Goss, of Stoke-on-Trent, who trained local people. William Gallimore, who had been Goss's chief modeller, made designs

79 Dublin lamp
standard, an expanded
version of the type
introduced in 1892.

80, 81 Miniature harps
of bog oak (coll. Mrs
Mary Boydell) and
Belleek ware, based on
a common model. The
Belleek harp dates from
c. 1875.

based on motifs from the Book of Kells before returning to England in 1866. A
local man, Michael Maguire, invented the now ubiquitous tea set design with sprays
of shamrock on a wicker background. The 'Shamrock' tea service had a scallop-
shell base, sprays of shamrock, and harp-shaped handles and finials. Belleek also
produced statuettes of Parian ware. One of the earliest showed 'Erin unveiling   82
her first Pot' – a cloth-draped urn – beside a harp and a broken Celtic cross.
It was modelled by William Boyton Kirk (1824–1900), one of a numerous family
of Dublin sculptors. The founders of the Belleek factory, an architect called Arm-
strong and McBirney, a Dublin businessman, died in 1884, and the factory was
taken over by a group of local men. The standard of workmanship remained high.
At the Paris Exhibition of 1900 they won a gold medal for a centrepiece in the
form of an urn with three harps on it and three wolfhounds round its base, the
whole decorated liberally with flowers.

By the end of the century it would have been difficult to turn around in Ireland
without being faced, in one form or another, by shamrocks, harps, round towers
and wolfhounds – on tea services, glass, jewellery, book covers, work-boxes, on
banners, in graveyards, and even, if you were a Catholic, in church. Although their
popularity lasted well into this century, and in some cases still survives, they began
to be regarded as suspect by the Celtic Renaissance generation of the turn of the
century: all four emblems as a group, and the shamrock by itself, were thought
to indicate a shallow, sentimental and ineffectual feeling for Ireland, or to symbolize
the lip-service paid to an Irish identity by the royal family and by the Viceroy
and Castle officials. Curiously enough, round towers or wolfhounds on their own
were acceptable. So were archaeological symbols like high crosses, Celtic interlace
and the 'Tara' Brooch, since they were reminders of Ireland's great cultural achievements of the past.

82 Belleek: *Erin
unveiling her first Pot*, a
matt and glazed Parian
figurine 45 cm. (18 in.)
high, modelled by
William Boyton Kirk
c. 1870 (Ulster Museum
Belfast).

CHAPTER 6

The Celtic Revival

THE GROWTH OF IRISH NATIONAL CONSCIOUSNESS in the nineteenth century had two phases. The first, with which we have been dealing, began with the development of interest in antiquities, and flowered in the Young Ireland movement. The feelings and ideas generated at that time had to last Ireland until almost the end of the century, and though they were gradually weakened and adulterated they formed the basis for the second phase, sometimes called the Irish Renaissance, or the Celtic Revival, which began to appear in the 1880s. Writing in 1902, John Millington Synge (1871–1909) said that if a young Trinity undergraduate in 1892 wanted to know more about Ireland, he had to learn from pamphlets picked up in second-hand book shops, from Grattan's speeches, Davis's poems, 'or the true history of Ireland from before the flood' (no doubt a reference to the romanticized histories which were so common in the nineteenth century), or he could go to the antiquarians, and read books like Stokes's *Life of Petrie*.[1] But already Standish O'Grady (1846–1915), Lady Gregory (1852–1932), Edward Martyn (1859–1923), Douglas 86 Hyde (1860–1949), W. B. Yeats (1865–1939) and George Russell, or AE (1867– 87 1935), had begun to work, though in obscurity, to provide fresh and stimulating 92 Irish literature. Although the new generation built on the old they also reacted 93 against it, and did not think very highly of its literary achievements.

The two revivals had several things in common. Both, though they involved Catholics, had their roots in the Protestant middle classes, both found their expression in literature, and both were closely bound up with politics and Ireland's freedom. Neither had much impact on the visual arts, though this was more obvious in the second phase than in the first. There were two reasons for this. When the poets and playwrights of the late nineteenth century wished to create a distinctively Irish literature, drawing on native sources, they found an unbroken tradition of folklore, rich in language and literary invention, which had remained alive in remoter country districts through several centuries of neglect. The people of the Irish-speaking districts, the *Gaeltacht*, had distinctly national music, dancing and storytelling, but no fine art to speak of, and very little appreciation of it. The last great period of Irish art, in the eighteenth century, was associated in people's minds with the Anglo-Irish Protestant Ascendancy, and therefore suspect among Nationalists.

Another reason for the Celtic Revival being mainly literary is that great literary talents, people like Yeats and Synge and Russell, consciously identified themselves with it. Even George Moore (1852–1933), who was already well established as a 90 novelist, and whose work drew very little on obviously Irish material, came back for a while to live in Dublin, painted his hall door green, and became involved

83 Jack B. Yeats: 'Will he catch them?', from *Life in the West of Ireland*, 1912.

84, 85 Jack B. Yeats:
'At the feis', and the
interior of a country
shop, from *Life in the
West of Ireland*, 1912.
Feiseanna, competitions
for singing, storytelling,
dancing or music
playing, were made
popular by the Gaelic
League.

in the Gaelic League. 'The Celt', he said, 'wants a Renaissance, and badly.'[2] Nothing of the sort happened among painters of the same generation, as we shall see (pp. 177 ff.). Walter Osborne, though he came of a Home Rule family, and moved in Nationalist circles, was not at all interested in politics. Nathaniel Hone just went on painting, and does not seem to have involved himself at all. John Lavery did not concern himself much with Ireland until about 1921, when the struggle was 141 nearly over. Orpen's work inspired by the Revival was savagely satirical, not at 142 all in the spirit of the movement. All of them painted in a broad European tradition, with a strong French influence, and there was nothing distinctively Irish about their work.

Of course, art did have some place. George Russell was a painter as well as a 86 poet, and sometimes inspired by a mystical vision of Ireland. It is to John Butler Yeats (1839–1922) as a portrait painter that we owe our knowledge of the appear- 92 ance of the leading literary figures. His son, Jack B. Yeats (1871–1957), working 93 in a highly personal manner, captured the people of the West of Ireland in paint, 83– and with pen and ink, in much the same way as Synge did in his plays. Apart from 85 the active production of sculpture or paintings, nearly everyone involved in politics and literature had to do with some organization dealing with art, most notably Hugh Lane's Gallery of Modern Art (see the next chapter). And in various branches of the applied arts Ireland produced work which in its beauty, its vigour, and its originality matched the literature of the period.

86 George Russell
(AE): *W. B. Yeats*,
pastel, 1903 (National
Gallery of Ireland).

87 Sarah Purser: *Edward Martyn* (Hugh Lane Municipal Gallery of Modern Art, Dublin). Artist and sitter were both involved in setting up the stained glass works An Túr Gloine.

The Celtic Revival took place on several widely-different cultural levels which overlapped because they had aims and impulses in common, and because they involved many of the same people. A remarkable number of organizations were founded, all concerned with one aspect or another of Irish culture. The Gaelic Athletics Association, founded by Michael Cusack in 1884, wanted to revive the ancient games and sports of Ireland. The National Literary Society, in which Yeats, Maud Gonne, and the old Fenian John O'Leary were involved, was founded in 1892. The Gaelic League was founded in 1893. Douglas Hyde – an Irish language scholar, and later first President of the Irish Free State – was one of its moving spirits, though the original idea had not been his.[3] Its object was the encouragement of the Irish language and of Irish culture. Father Jeremiah O'Donovan summed up its ideals in a lecture in 1902:[4]

> The Gaelic League, as I see it, aims at the creation of an Irish Ireland. It hopes to accomplish this by the spread of true national ideas. Once those ideas are grasped, a development of Ireland from within, embracing language, literature, art, industries and music will necessarily follow.

It held a festival each year, the *Oireachtas*, with literary prizes and competitions for Irish songs and dancing. Though by 1906 the Gaelic League had an art committee, and held craft exhibitions, it was not really much concerned with the fine arts – perhaps for the reason suggested earlier, that it was difficult to associate them with a Celtic past – and an article in the League's magazine, *An Claidheamh Soluis* (The Sword of Light), in November 1904 admitted as much.[5] An even stronger indication is to be got from Douglas Hyde's evidence before the Royal Commission on Irish University Education in 1902.[6] He is being interviewed by Professor John Rhys and Mr Justice Madden.

IV Sarah Purser: detail of a window in Loughrea Cathedral, Co. Galway, showing St Brendan. See p. 156.

Rhys: ... I suppose you would regard the Gaelic League movement as one much more comprehensive than one merely referring to the language and literature?
Hyde: Yes.
Rhys: You would regard it in a large aspect as a development of the self respect of a nation?
Hyde: Entirely so.
Rhys: You also take in ... Irish amusements, Irish music, and other things connected with the national life?
Hyde: Yes.
Rhys: Then also, last, but not by any means least, you would take in Irish art?
Hyde: That also.
Rhys: ... Don't you think, with all the artistic talent of the Irish – they have undoubtedly had a very great artistic talent in times past – that a School of Art might be developed in Ireland as part of its educational system?
Hyde: Yes. As you have mentioned that I may say that we have established now in Dublin a school for the production of Irish art glass, which I think will at least equal, and probably beat the continental school, and it is interesting, from my point of view, to remark that the man mainly responsible for the establishment of that school is a product of the Gaelic League, Mr Edward Martyn of Tillyra Castle, who, having become a Gaelic Leaguer, and learned to read Irish, took a chief part in establishing this school. ...
Rhys: In any case Ireland, and more especially Catholic Ireland, is a large purchaser of this artistic commodity, and could very well produce it itself, if its artistic instincts were trained; do you think so?
Hyde: That is so. ...
Rhys: Something has been done in the past, but I don't know that it has been altogether successful, in regard to Irish crosses and so on. I suppose that that is capable of development.
Hyde: I hope it will develop in the future, but I don't think it has developed much up to the present.
Rhys: I occasionally see Irish crosses brought to England, but they are not always a success, perhaps they are not always the best specimens?
Hyde: They are done by bad workmen. They are done by plumb and line instead of freehand. The old Irish crosses were freehand, and always looked beautiful, but they are now done by rule.
Rhys: All that would come in under this comprehensive movement, and more or less under the purview of the Gaelic League?
Hyde: It all more or less would.

What emerges from this exchange is that Hyde is not interested in art, and knows very little about it. It is Rhys who keeps the conversation going, and Hyde only really kindles to the part played by the Gaelic League in Edward Martyn's achievement. Otherwise his answers are laconic in the extreme. This seems to be typical of the League in general. Except for their support for Lane's gallery they were only interested in certain aspects of applied art. Given the economic situation of Ireland at the time this was reasonable: applied art could help in the improvement of cottage industries in rural areas. And, as we saw in the last chapter, it could also go back for inspiration to the great early medieval period, and be more obviously Irish than painting or sculpture.

The Irish Agricultural Organisation Society, founded by Sir Horace Plunkett, though mainly interested in farming, became involved in cottage industries, which could bring added prosperity to poor country districts.[7] Its headquarters were in Plunkett House, Merrion Square, Dublin, and one of its principal organizers was George Russell, who edited its magazine, *The Irish Homestead*, and as a painter pro-

v   Painted vault over the crossing in Letterkenny Cathedral, Co. Donegal. In the roundels are the cathedral's patron, St Adhamhnan, and St Columcille. See p. 131.

87

92

vided another link with the visual arts. He was involved with Eastern mysticism and the Theosophical Society, and would wander in the hills seeing visions of mystical beings from Celtic mythology. Some people affected to think that these visions looked like a pantomime fairy, with tulle dress, glittery crown, and wand – as in Max Beerbohm's cartoon, *Mr W. B. Yeats presenting Mr George Moore to the Queen of the Fairies* (Hugh Lane Municipal Gallery of Modern Art, Dublin). Because of this mystical association, and also because Plunkett and Russell and other leading organizers of the agricultural co-operative movement had beards, they were known in Dublin as 'the hairy fairies of Plunkett House'.[8]

Out of the Plunkett House organization came the impetus which set up the Department of Agriculture and Technical Instruction for Ireland in 1899.[9] Sir Horace Plunkett was its first Vice-President, and T. P. Gill its Secretary. It took over, among other duties, responsibility for the School of Art in Dublin. It has always been something of a joke, and an Irish joke at that, that art education should have been the responsibility of a Department of Agriculture, but at the time it was a sensible arrangement, since the school was mainly concerned with design for industry and the training of craftsmen. It had begun in the eighteenth century as the Drawing School of the Dublin Society, but came, in 1849, under the heavy hand of the Department of Science and Art at South Kensington in London, anxious to centralize art education and improve design standards in the British Isles. This ruined the school as a training ground for painters, sculptors and even architects, but it was good for crafts. In the 1880s and 1890s it did a lot to develop lace and crochet in poor districts. In the years after it came under the Department of Agriculture and Technical Instruction it was an active participant in the Arts and Crafts revival, setting up classes in stained glass under A. E. Child in 1903, and later bringing in Oswald Reeves to teach enamelling and metalwork (see pp. 155, 163).

The Abbey Theatre was perhaps the most important cultural foundation of the period, and its contribution is too well known to need repetition. Like the Gaelic League it was only peripherally involved in the visual arts, for example in costume and set design. Even here there were limits to the lengths they were prepared to go to for authentic national costume, and the pampooties, or hide slippers, for *Riders to the Sea* were made in Dublin, not brought from Aran, because, said Lady Gregory, there was no point in bringing local smells into the theatre.[10] The company also employed important members of the Arts and Crafts movement to decorate its headquarters, the Abbey Theatre, when it opened, using stained glass from the co-operative workshop *An Túr Gloine* (The Tower of Glass: see p. 156), and copper mirror frames from the new metal-works at Youghal.[11] Apart from that members of the company threw themselves into the effort to raise money for Hugh Lane's Gallery of Modern Art.

The various mystical groups, the Hermetic Society in its different avatars, and the Irish Theosophical Society, seem even more peripheral to the visual arts, and irrelevant to the national revival. They were linked to them, however, through the involvement of people like W. B. Yeats and AE, who wished to draw on native mysticism and visions of a Celtic past. The 'hairy fairies', Eastern mysticism, and nationalism were certainly confused in the popular mind, as witness *The Irish Builder* on 29 August 1901: 'Let our young men and maidens compose mystic verses savouring of Bhudism, and converse in what we have no manner of doubt is execrably

142

86
92

bad Irish ... and there is Ireland regenerated.' *The Irish Builder*, which was not a highbrow magazine, was not, of course, serious. It believed that Ireland's redemption lay in the inculcation of sound commercial principles.

The Dublin United Arts Club was founded in 1905, to bring together people interested in art and to 'crystallize the renaissance movement then going on in Dublin'. Its secretary was Ellen Duncan, who was Curator of Hugh Lane's Gallery, and who sent accounts of Dublin exhibitions to *The Studio*. W. B. Yeats was a member, as was his brother Jack, the painter. Constance Markievicz, the 'rebel Countess' of 1916, and her husband Casimir, both of whom had studied painting at the Académie Julian in Paris, joined. So did the Orpens – William, the painter, and his brother Richard, an architect – as well as AE and Percy French, who is remembered for his music-hall Irish songs, but who also painted rather watery Irish bogland views. The club seems to have cultivated, in those days, a bohemian atmosphere:[12]

> If you long for things artistic,
> If you revel in the nebulous and mystic,
> If your hair's too long
> And your tie's all wrong
> And your speech is symbolistic;
> If your tastes are democratic
> And your mode of life's essentially erratic;
> If you seek success
> From no fixed address,
> But you sleep in someone's attic,
>   Join the Arts Club,
>   Join the Arts Club.

What is interesting about the spirit of regeneration in Ireland, the Celtic Revival, is that it even permeated what was, naturally enough, a bastion of English culture, the viceregal court. This is particularly true of the two periods in office, in 1886 and 1906–15, of the Earl of Aberdeen.[13] The Aberdeens arrived predisposed to Home Rule (they were close friends of Gladstone), and, in the case of Ishbel, Lady Aberdeen, with that romantic partiality for Ireland to which some English people are prone. They were kind, practical, and humanitarian, and set about doing what they could to improve conditions for the poor, and to forge as many links as possible with Irish, and not just Ascendancy, society. In fact they seem to have alienated the Ascendancy. 'Many people of breeding gave up all idea of going to the Castle', said one hostile critic. 'Without being a snob, it was no pleasure, and rather embarrassing to meet the lady at dinner who had measured you for your shirts the week before.'[14] When Lord Aberdeen was appointed Viceroy, Lady Aberdeen had thrown herself into the project of going to Ireland with the headlong enthusiasm which was characteristic of her, and prepared to make the State Entry into Dublin with her children dressed in green velvet coats. This was vetoed by officials, since *The Wearing of the Green* was a popular song at the time, and had unmistakably Nationalist connotations ('for they're hangin' men and women for the wearin' of the green'). The children were dressed in white Irish poplin instead and the green coats were sent to be dyed blue.[15] By the time of her farewell levee, a year later, she had learnt to be more circumspect, and her dress was of St Patrick's blue poplin (an 'Irish' colour without unfortunate associations) and her bonnet trimmed with

rose, thistle and shamrock. There is an interesting portrait of the Aberdeens' children painted at this period: called *Two Little Home Rulers*, it shows Dudley and Archie 88 Gordon, in knee breeches, buckled shoes, and tail coats (the old-fashioned dress of the Irish peasant), sitting in a wheelbarrow full of potatoes, against a wild and mountainy landscape.

The official attitude continued to relax in the next few years. In 1899 Lady Betty Balfour, wife of the Chief Secretary, put on a series of tableaux from Yeats's play *The Countess Cathleen*.[16] Yeats himself refused to help, on the grounds that he could 89 not go into the house of a Government official, but she managed to enlist an associate of his, T. W. Rolleston, and George Coffey, Keeper of Antiquities in the National Museum. Coffey took part in the tableau, and was also, presumably, responsible for borrowing the Celtic gold ornaments from the museum which Lady Fingall, who played the Countess Cathleen, wore, according to her own account, at her waist and in her hair. The collection of Celtic treasures in the National Museum was the one which Petrie had been so active in assembling for the Royal Irish Academy: it was transferred on loan after the Museum opened in 1890.

By the time of the Aberdeens' second term of office, in 1906, the atmosphere had changed considerably from the shamrockery of their first, and they set about, in their energetic way, changing it more. Lady Aberdeen continued her work for the Irish Industries Association, which she had founded in 1886 to promote and sell the products of Irish cottage industries. Guests at the Viceregal Ball of 1907 were expected to wear Irish lace – dresses in the case of the women, cuffs and jabots in the case of the men.[17] Both Ishbel Aberdeen and her husband were interested in town planning, and they invited Patrick Geddes, a pioneer in that field, to bring his Town Planning Exhibition to Dublin in 1911.[18] Lord Aberdeen offered a prize of £500 for a town plan of Dublin. They did not stay on entirely neutral ground. Before her return to Dublin Lady Aberdeen had become a member of the Irish

Literary Society in London, a group of which Yeats was a founder.[19] She would have liked to go to plays at the Abbey, but couldn't, as the players would not perform before the Viceroy and his Lady, nor treat them as private persons. They did, however, give a St Patrick's Night ball in Dublin Castle when 'members of the Gaelic League came and danced along with officers of the Royal Irish Rifles in sets of the Connaught Jig'.[20] Not only that, but 'a still more daring surprise awaited a select party drawn from both north and south, old and new nobility, in an all-Irish evening, when the whole entertainment, – authors, performers, instruments – were of the country, when songs in Gaelic were heard in the castle for the first time'. They also put on a play, *Finn and his Companions*, by Standish O'Grady, in the open air, at a garden-party in the grounds of the Viceregal Lodge.[21] Irish dancing seems to have been taken up at the time by Castle society. Lady Fingall says in her memoirs that she 'learnt to dance jigs in the Irish Renaissance, at Killeen, when I and the children and the governess had had an expert – the blacksmith from Dunshaughlin – to instruct us'.[22]

When the Aberdeens left Ireland in 1915 Lord Aberdeen was offered a marquisate, and to commemorate their stay he and his wife chose the additional title of Tara. There was immediate indignation at this: however well disposed they were, it was tactless of them to have chosen a name which, as the ancient seat of the High Kings of Ireland, was sacred to Irishmen. They eventually compromised, and adopted Aberdeen and Temair, an approximation of the Irish spelling of Tara, *Teamhair*.

The penetration of viceregal society by the Celtic Renaissance was, no doubt, on a very superficial level. For Nationalists the Castle remained the Castle, a symbol of English tyranny in Ireland. It is, however, an indication of the strength of the Revival that it infiltrated even into the milieu which had dedicated itself, in earlier years, to keeping distinctively Irish cultural achievements to a minimum.

89 A tableau from Yeats's play *The Countess Cathleen*, 1899. Lady Fingall, as Cathleen, is seated on the ground; the man standing on the right is wearing 'Celtic' costume, with a *brat* held on his shoulders by Celtic brooches (see p. 148).

CHAPTER 7

Hugh Lane and the Gallery of Modern Art

AS FAR AS THE FINE ARTS WERE CONCERNED, the most conspicuous, and lasting, manifestation of the Celtic Revival was not a single work of painting or sculpture, but an art gallery. It was to house not just Irish art but also the best contemporary European work. In retrospect its close connection with the Revival is obvious. Its founder, Hugh Lane (1875–1915), was a nephew of Lady Gregory. She, and the 91 Abbey Players, threw themselves into the effort to raise money for it. Yeats, Synge, 93 Moore, Martyn, and many others worked for it and wrote about it. The Gaelic 86 League was also enthusiastic. Even at the time it was recognized as an important 87 part of the Revival. Lady Gregory, in an article called 'A Stone of the Building' in *The Freeman's Journal* for 13 December 1904, connected the gallery specifically with the movement. She regarded the Gaelic League as the cornerstone of the building that was the new Ireland. Many more stones had been added: the school of Irish learning, the *Feis Ceoil* (a festival of music competitions), the National Theatre Society (the Abbey Theatre); and now, she wrote of the proposed collection, 'no one could doubt that the possession of these pictures and the influence they must have on our own young students will be an advance in the dignity of our country in its place among nations, a worthy building-stone laid upon its wall'. At the time of the opening of the gallery, in 1908, an editorial in *An Claidheamh Soluis*, the Gaelic League magazine, said that 'such an event is in kind as real a manifestation of the new life which is commencing to surge through the veins of Ireland as is a *Feis* in an Irish-speaking countryside or a new novel from the pen of An tAthair 84 Peadar Ua Laoghaire' (Father Peter O'Leary, a major figure in the language movement).[1]

Hugh Lane was the son of Augusta Gregory's sister, Adelaide Persse, and a clergyman from Co. Cork called Lane.[2] He developed an early liking for the arts, and in 1893 was sent to work for Colnaghi's, the art dealers, in London. He showed an extraordinary aptitude for the business – his perceptive eye for a picture was always one of his greatest talents – and in 1898 he set up on his own account. His interest was in old masters rather than in modern paintings, and in 1902 he got together the Winter Exhibition of Old Masters at the Royal Hibernian Academy. It seems to have been at this time that he was drawn into the cultural life of Dublin, though he probably knew all the leading figures already. He had met W. B. Yeats at Coole Park, Lady Gregory's house in Co. Galway, in 1900.

Early in 1904, at very short notice, he was asked by the Department of Agriculture and Technical Instruction to organize an exhibition of Irish art to be sent to the Louisiana Purchase Exposition at St Louis, Missouri. He threw himself into the project with his usual energy, and was then told that the insurance was too high, and

90 William Orpen: *Homage to Manet*, 1909 (City Art Gallery, Manchester). Seated below Manet's *Eva Gonzales*, which Hugh Lane had bought in 1905, are George Moore, P. Wilson Steer, Henry Tonks, and Lane himself. D. S. MacColl and Walter Sickert stand behind.

91 John Singer Sargent: *Hugh Lane*, presented to Lane in 1906 'in recognition of his unselfish and untiring efforts to establish a gallery of Modern Art for Ireland' (Hugh Lane Municipal Gallery of Modern Art, Dublin).

92 John Butler Yeats: *George Russell (AE)*, 1903, commissioned by Hugh Lane (National Gallery of Ireland). Russell was deeply involved in the Celtic Revival as a writer and painter, and also as a member of the co-operative movement and editor of its magazine *The Irish Homestead*.

that the exhibition could not go. He decided that since people had put themselves to inconvenience to lend the pictures, and since he himself had worked very hard on the project, the pictures should be shown in any case, at an exhibition which opened at the Guildhall in London in May 1904.[3] So great was his enthusiasm to assemble a body of Irish painting that he stretched the definition of Irish to its furthest limits, and even beyond, including as he did Gordon Craig, Mark Fisher, and Charles Shannon, who had been able to rake up an Irish grandmother. Apart from that the selection was representative of the range and richness of Irish painting at the time, and drew a very favourable response from the press.

The idea of a gallery of modern art for Dublin had been in the air for some time. Lane had acquired paintings by Nathaniel Hone at the joint exhibition of Hone and John Butler Yeats in the autumn of 1901, from Yeats he commissioned portraits 92 of Irish personalities (including Lady Gregory and AE),[4] and after the Royal Hiber- 93 nian Academy retrospective exhibition of the work of Walter Osborne, in the winter of 1903–04, he bought several of the pictures. It was in the preface to the catalogue of the Guildhall Exhibition that Lane crystallized the idea of a modern art gallery:[5]

93 John Butler Yeats: *Augusta, Lady Gregory*, 1903, commissioned by Hugh Lane, her nephew (National Gallery of Ireland).

There are so many painters of Irish birth or Irish blood in the first rank at this moment, that extreme interest is being taken in this bringing together of sufficient specimens of their work to enable students of art to discover what common or race quantities appear through it. There is something of common race instinct in the work of all original Irish writers of today, and it can hardly be absent in the sister art.

He added that there was a need for a gallery of Irish and modern art in Dublin, that such a gallery would be necessary to the student if there was to be a distinct school of painting in Ireland, for it is one's contemporaries that teach one the most.

Though Lane was right when he said that Irish writing of the day had something of a 'common race instinct', he was being optimistic in supposing that the same was true of painting. In the first place he spread his net too wide, and included people with little Irish heritage and very varied backgrounds. In the second place, even among those painters who were undoubtedly Irish there was very little of the common purpose and community of ideas which animated the writers of the time.

In 1904 Lane got wind of the sale of the collection of the recently deceased Staats Forbes, which consisted mostly of nineteenth-century French paintings, and arranged with the executors to exhibit about one hundred and sixty of them in Dublin, to raise money for their purchase for the proposed gallery.[6] To them he added a selection of paintings obtained, on similar terms, from Durand-Ruel, the Paris dealer famous for his support of the Impressionists. He also added pictures he himself was prepared to present, and some promised by artists if a gallery were founded in Dublin. These were all exhibited in the winter of 1904–05, first at the Royal Hibernian Academy and then, after a month, at the National Museum of Ireland. A large number of the pictures were bought, either by individuals who paid for them and presented them, or with money collected and subscribed by various groups. Among the individual patrons were the Prince and Princess of Wales, on a state visit to Dublin. President Theodore Roosevelt sent a cheque, saying that he 'believed this gallery would be an important step towards giving Dublin the position it by rights should have'.[7]

The exhibition was also the occasion of the first of the rows which were to dog the history of the modern art gallery, about the authenticity of a picture attributed to Corot. This was partly justified by the quality of the picture, and scholarship has since suggested that its critics were right, but at the time feelings ran very high. It was pointed out that the Corot, supposed to have been the first one he exhibited, bore a close resemblance to a landscape by the Hungarian artist Géza Mészöly, painted in 1877. The Director of the National Museum, Colonel Plunkett, who did not approve of the pictures, and who had said at the opening of the Guildhall Exhibition that he hoped never to see a picture hung in Dublin until the artist had been dead a hundred years, fixed a photograph of the Mészöly to the wall above the 'Corot', implying that the latter was a sketch for it. There was great indignation among Lane's supporters, especially as Plunkett had plainly acted out of spite. John Shawe-Taylor, Lane's cousin, went into the Museum with a screwdriver and removed the offending photograph. He was then taken, by Lane, to lunch at the Viceregal Lodge, so that he could confess his crime to the Lord Lieutenant, and be forgiven, before an official complaint could be received.[8]

Lane, though he inspired loyalty and affection in large numbers of people, also had many enemies. He was mistrusted because he was a picture dealer, and it was whispered that he had made a lot of money as a result of the Guildhall Exhibition, and that he would also get a commission if the Staats Forbes collection were bought in Dublin. It is true that he made an enormous fortune by dealing, but the generosity with which he spent it on pictures for public galleries ought to have silenced criticism. He was touchy, and impatient of bureaucracy, and made enemies among officials like Plunkett. He was mistrusted in some Nationalist circles, and his preoccupation with the arts, his aesthetic tastes, made him an object of suspicion among the fox-hunting gentry. Most of all, he was mistrusted, as people so often are in Dublin, because he was energetic and successful, and went ahead and got things done.

Among his major achievements was the Municipal Gallery of Modern Art, which opened in Clonmell House, Harcourt Street, in January 1908. The collection included the works from the Staats Forbes collection, paintings by Corot, Troyon, Fantin Latour, Harpignies, Degas, Millet, Daumier and Constable.[9] It also included

pictures given by painters. Lane presented a group of portraits of contemporary Irishmen and women, Rodin's bronze *L'Age d'Airain*, and his collection of contemporary British paintings and drawings. He lent his collection of modern French pictures, which he intended to present to the gallery when it had a more permanent building. There were thirty-nine of them, and they included Renoir's *Les Parapluies*, Manet's *Eva Gonzales* and *Concert aux Tuileries*, Degas' *La Plage*, a Pissarro view 90
of Louveciennes, a Monet view of Vétheuil and Puvis de Chavannes' *Décollation de St Jean Baptiste*. There were also paintings by Courbet, Corot, Daumier, even an Ingres and a Gérôme. It was a distinguished and representative collection of nineteenth-century French painting, remarkable for its time.

The gallery was praised and hailed on all sides. John B. Yeats had said of the collection, when it was exhibited in 1904, that if it were to become the permanent possession of Ireland it would do more for the education of the people than a Catholic university.[10] Synge wrote about the gallery, and linked it to the renaissance in literature.[11] When it opened the Gaelic League magazine devoted articles to it in both Irish and English.[12] The Irish one praised the fact that the name of the gallery, and the titles of the rooms, were in Irish as well as in English. The article in English said it was a sign of the new life that was beginning to surge through Ireland, and that Mr Lane and the Gaelic League were allies: they were bringing back the poet and the *seanchaidhe* (storyteller), he the painter and the sculptor. The gallery would ensure that young Irish artists became familiar with modern European art, and that the public would also be made familiar with it, so that the young artists would be understood. An 'art atmosphere' would develop in Dublin, and a school of artists would grow up whose work would be an authentic expression of the soul of Ireland, because it would be created by artists who were in a genuine sense Irish. The magazine *Sinn Féin* (We Ourselves) wrote on 4 January 1908 that the gallery 'whilst adding to the education and enjoyment of our fellow citizens at large' would 'greatly enhance the prestige of our native city'. The gallery had some opponents. George Moore, though he later supported it with as much enthusiasm as other right-minded people, began, with his usual perversity, by opposing it, in a letter dated 29 June 1903 to the Dublin newspapers:

> The establishment of a permanent art gallery in Dublin will increase this waste of public money; it will certainly establish some more officials in Dublin, and we have enough officials here and to spare. It will establish a standard of false art in the country, and will lead to any amount of intrigue and misapplication of money. The late Walter Osborne used to speak to me with horror of Mr Lane's project, and knowing Dublin well he was able to draw pictures of the intrigues that would soon be set afoot by painters of Irish scenery and by painters of incidents in Irish history to induce the Corporation to buy their pictures.

Another, and more permanent enemy was William Murphy, newspaper owner, Chairman of Dublin Tramways, a bitter opponent of trade unionism, a singularly unpleasant person. His paper, the *Irish Independent*, had published an article on the proposed gallery on 16 January 1903, praising Lane's efforts. Practical steps needed to be taken to establish a genuine school of native art in Dublin, and the paper had long pointed out the decadence of the annual exhibitions in the Royal Hibernian Academy. 'To find a picture containing a story, or depicting anything dramatic or interesting, has been rare.' The paper had doubts about 'modern art', however, and did not believe that what Ireland needed for the creation of a genuine school of native art was the 'wholesale importation of the works of alien painters'. The stores of Celtic legend and Celtic song, the dark 'but sometimes lightsome' pages of the history of Ireland could afford plenty of subjects, for example 'the scene when the conquered banners of the English were laid on the altar steps of Limerick Cathedral at the feet of Rinuccini'. For the *Irish Independent* it might still have been 1840. For Lane and his friends, who had cosmopolitan ideas about art, an Irish School was no longer a matter of patriotic subjects, but of common stylistic qualities.

After the gallery opened in 1908 Lane went on working for it, acquiring new pictures and re-hanging others, seeking publicity, but most of all agitating for the building of a permanent home for the collection, as the Harcourt Street house was only a temporary measure. It was that which led to the most epic row of all, one

94 'Sir Hugh Lane producing masterpieces for Dublin', Max Beerbohm's view in 1909 of Lane casting pearls before Paudeen and Biddy: see p. 114 (Hugh Lane Municipal Gallery of Modern Art, Dublin).

which lost Lane's French pictures to Dublin. The row was about the choice of site for the new gallery, about who should design it, and about whether the Corporation would put up money for it, and if so how much. It was very complicated, involving numerous factions and sub-factions, and dragging in politics, religion, and industrial relations. Nearly all of Dublin's leading citizens, including major figures in the Renaissance, became involved.

In 1912 Lane began to remind the Corporation of Dublin about the conditions of his loan of the French pictures, and in January 1913 it voted £22,000, provided a site could be found and the balance of the cost, estimated at £43,000, could be found elsewhere. Once again people began writing to the papers, and collecting money. The Five Provinces Branch of the Gaelic League instituted a shilling collection.[13] The Abbey Players gave a private performance of Bernard Shaw's play *The Shewing up of Blanco Posnet* at the Court Theatre, London, to pay off the £1,000 they had guaranteed towards the cost of a gallery building. The play had been banned by the Lord Chamberlain, which prompted *The Times* to remark, 'if it is ever proper to do evil that good may come ... the presentation of Mr Shaw's horse-stealing melodrama ... was abundantly justified by the excellence of the cause for which the matinee was given.'[14] Lady Gregory, on tour in the United States with the Abbey Players, raised money, and got promises of a great deal more. Bernard Shaw sent a hundred guineas, and a letter in which he said:[15]

> Sir Hugh Lane, in making a great collection of the modern French School that arose at the same time as the English School, and of the work of those painters, especially Irish painters, who assimilated its technical discoveries, and responded to that French audacity of spirit which is so congenial to our own national temperament, has placed in the hands of the Corporation of Dublin an instrument of culture, the value of which is far beyond anything that can be expressed in figures by the city accountant.

He added that the taste and knowledge which he had acquired as a boy in the National Gallery in Dublin had made it possible for him to live by his pen without discrediting his country, and was built into the fabric of the best work he had done.

In contrast to the generosity evident from these various efforts, there was also a certain amount of haggling by people who felt that the Corporation should pay the whole cost, and by others who thought that all of the money should be subscribed from private sources, and Corporation funds spent on urgent matters such as housing for the poor. There were others still who thought that there should be a large public subscription, as evidence, in hard cash, that the people of Ireland as a whole wanted a gallery of modern art in Dublin. It was this body of opinion which prompted Yeats's poem 'The Gift', published in the Dublin newspapers on 11 January 1913, and addressed 'To a friend who promises a bigger subscription than his first to the Dublin Municipal Gallery if the amount collected proves that there is a considerable "popular demand" for the pictures'.[16]

> You gave, but will not give again
> Until enough of Paudeen's pence
> By Biddy's half-pennies have lain
> To be 'some sort of evidence,'
> Before you've put your guineas down,
> That things, it were a pride to give,
> Are what the blind and ignorant town
> Imagines best to make it thrive.

What cared Duke Ercole, that bid
His mummers to the market-place,
What th' onion sellers thought or did
So that his Plutarch set the pace
For the Italian comedies?
And Guidobaldo when he made
That grammar school of courtesies
Where wit and beauty learned their trade,
Upon Urbino's windy hill,
Had sent no runners to and fro
That he might learn the shepherds' will; ...

Your open hand but shows our loss
For he knew better how to live.
Leave Paudeens to their pitch and toss;
Look up in the sun's eye, and give
What the exultant heart calls good,
That some new day may breed the best
Because you gave, not what they would,
But the right twigs for an eagle's nest.

This poem expresses some of the complexities of the time, its implicit belief in the
Irish Renaissance combining with bitterness about certain elements of Irish society.
Its arrogant dismissal of Paudeen (the Irish philistine) and his like seems extreme,
until one looks, for example, at the newspaper correspondence about the Lane
gallery.

While money was being collected for the gallery building, debates were going
on about a possible site and architect. Lane himself chose the very distinguished
English architect, Edwin Lutyens (1869–1944). Objections were raised because he
was not Irish, though it was pointed out that his mother was. There was also a
certain amount of resentment among the architectural profession, because Richard
Orpen had helped Lane to look for a site, and even made some plans, and it was

95 Edwin Lutyens:
design for the
Municipal Gallery in
Dublin on a bridge
over the Liffey, *c.* 1913
(Hugh Lane Municipal
Gallery of Modern Art,
Dublin).

felt that the commission should have gone to him.[17] However there was no one in Ireland at the time of Lutyens's stature, or, as Yeats expressed it in his patronizing way, 'we have no Irish architect whom anybody suspects of remarkable talent'.[18] Besides, Lutyens had offered to design the building, and a garden round it, in exchange for an old master – and, in any case, Lane was determined to have him.

The battle of the sites was more heated still, and there was no lack of conflicting ideas. Earlsfort Terrace, beside the new National University, was proposed: Yeats liked the idea of the students wandering in and out between lectures, but Lane had seen designs for the university building, and would not put a beautiful building beside such an ugly one.[19] The old Turkish Baths in Lincoln Place were suggested, an exotic building of horseshoe arches and onion domes, and Orpen made plans for their conversion, but the proposal came to nothing.[20] Lutyens made designs for a long, low, porticoed building in St Stephen's Green, but this site was turned down by Lord Ardilaun, who had presented the Green as a park to the city. His reason, according to William Murphy, still a fierce enemy of any proposal to build a gallery, was that 'fresh air was a more desirable asset for the people than French art'.[21]

The most exciting scheme, and one which caught the imagination of many, was for a building across the Liffey below O'Connell Bridge, on the site of the Metal Bridge, which it was proposed anyhow to demolish. Lane was very keen on the idea, and so was Lutyens, who made a very attractive design. Yeats also was in favour: he abandoned his dream of the students wandering in and out, and visualized instead the common people of Dublin (he had met a house painter who appreciated Mancini). The bridge site would also have solved the problem of having to buy land for the building. But there was opposition to this idea as well. William Murphy was, as usual, vocal in his opposition. He said that Lutyens would not dare to erect such a building over the Thames, and that by building it in Dublin he was trying his architectural experiment out 'on the dog'.[22]

In the event the Corporation, having accepted the bridge scheme, changed its mind, and also decided against an English architect. Other sites were once again suggested, but Lane was determined to have Lutyens and the bridge, and, in a fury, removed his French pictures from the Harcourt Street gallery. There was consternation among his friends and supporters, and the public at large. Dublin paper sellers on 31 July 1913 had placards saying in huge black letters: 'SIR H. LANE TO REMOVE THE PICTURES AT ONCE. REMARKABLE INTERVIEW'. Once again there was a burst of newspaper articles and letters. The Trades Council published a resolution calling on the Aldermen and Councillors to accept Lane's offer.[23] They said that it was their opinion that the foul methods resorted to by the opposition to the erection of a gallery were worthy of their chief instigators (Murphy, in fact), whose main concern was to insult Lane so that he would take the pictures away, their aim being to deny the working man access to avenues of advancement and to limit the opportunities of unemployed men getting useful work.

When Lane removed his pictures he gave the Corporation six weeks to accept Lutyens's design. The question was debated in the middle of September 1913, and his terms were rejected by a majority of seven. On 19 September Lane wrote to the *Irish Times*, saying that the French paintings were to go to the National Gallery in London, and the rest of his collection on loan to Belfast.[24] He made a new will,

95

VI–XI Dun Emer Guild: banners in Loughrea Cathedral, designed by Jack B. Yeats and his wife and embroidered in 1902–03 by Lily Yeats and her assistants. From left to right, starting at the top, they show St Cainnigh, St Ita (with the infant St Brendan), St Columcille (whose bookmark is in the form of a Celtic cross), St Iarfhlaith or Jarlath, St Eanna or Enda, and St Brendan in his ship. See p. 157.

naoṁ Cainniġ

naoṁ Íte

naoṁ Colum Cille

naoṁ Iarflaiṫ

naoṁ Éanna

naoṁ Breandán

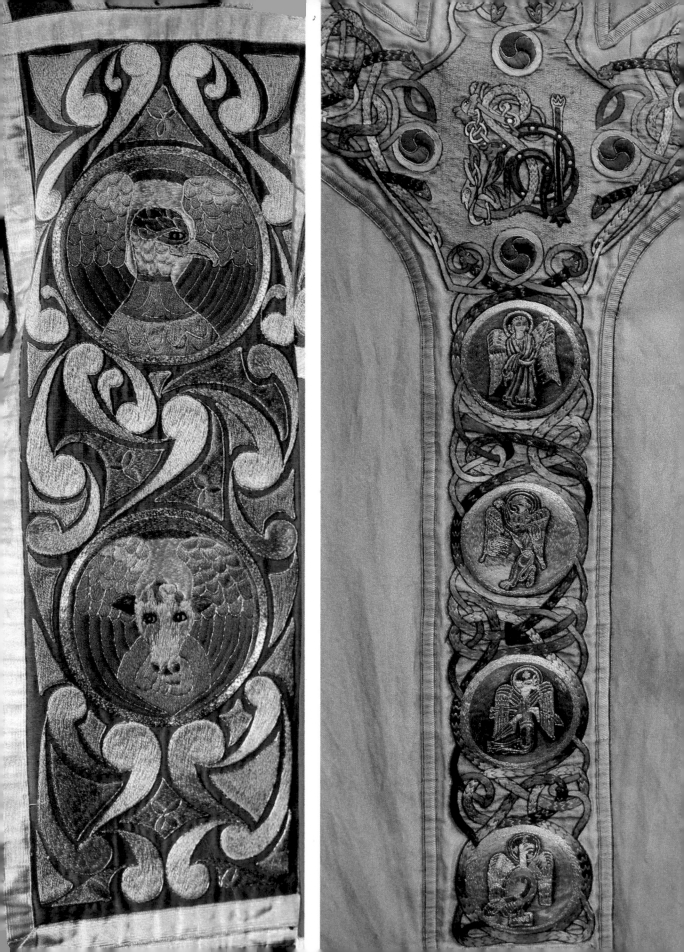

dated 11 October 1913, in which he bequeathed his French pictures to the National Gallery to form the basis of a collection of modern Continental art, adding:[25]

> I hope this alteration from the Modern Gallery to the National Gallery will be remembered by the Dublin Municipality and others as an example of its want of public spirit in the year 1913, and of the folly of such bodies assuming to decide on questions of Art instead of relying on expert opinion.

Not that the National Gallery treated him very much better. Having accepted the loan, and agreed to show the pictures, the Trustees then said they would only hang a selection, fifteen.[26] In the meantime Lane had been made Director of the National Gallery in Dublin, and began to look more kindly again on the Municipal Gallery. On 3 February 1915, on the eve of a trip to the United States, he added a codicil to the earlier will, revoking the bequest to the London gallery, and leaving the pictures to Dublin, on condition that a suitable building was provided for them within five years of his death. Unfortunately, he failed to have it witnessed. Just three months later, early in May 1915, he died when the *Lusitania*, on which he was returning from New York, was torpedoed off the coast of Cork.

His French pictures were in London, and a campaign was mounted, with Lady Gregory in charge, to get them back. But the unwitnessed codicil had no legal force, and the London officials, when asked to give the paintings back, said they were waiting for advice from their lawyers.[27] The question dragged on, and public feeling in Dublin was once again aroused. In London the matter was brought up by successive waves of politicians and debated in the Commons and in the Lords. Finally, in 1924, by which time the Irish Free State had been set up, a British Parliamentary Committee was appointed to look into the matter. Its report, presented to Parliament in June 1926, concluded that Lane had thought he was making a legal disposition, and intended the pictures to go to Ireland.[28] However, they did not feel that the legal defect should be remedied by legislation, on the grounds that Dublin had done nothing since Lane's death to build a gallery (how could it, when the matter of the will had not been settled?), and that had Lane seen the new Tate Gallery building in London he would have destroyed the codicil. The report was both unfair and illogical, and the pictures remained in London.

xII Dun Emer Guild: detail of the front of a chasuble embroidered for Loughrea Cathedral, incorporating the symbols of St John and St Luke. See p. 157.

xIII Barry Egan: detail of the back of a cloth-of-gold chasuble made for the Honan Chapel, Cork, in 1916. The embroidery, designed by Ethel Josephine Scally, includes symbols of the Evangelists that are taken (like those of the Dun Emer dossal, ill. xIV) from the Book of Kells. See p. 165.

In 1933 the Municipal Gallery moved from Harcourt Street to Charlemont House, Parnell Square, a Georgian town house converted for the purpose. Room was reserved for the French pictures, and from time to time the matter was raised by different Irish Governments, and brought up again in the Commons and Lords. Eventually, in 1959, the two Governments came to an arrangement under which the collection would be divided, and half of it shown for five years in each country, though the pictures in Dublin are, technically, only on loan. This arrangement is due for reassessment.

It is clear from the testimony of Lane's friends and impartial observers that he intended his pictures to go to Dublin. His bequest of them to the National Gallery was made in a moment of anger, and was also probably intended to force Dublin Corporation into some sort of action. Morally, if not according to the strictly applied letter of the law, they belong to Ireland, and, in the words of one commentator, 'Any decent private individual presented with the same problem would return the pictures to Dublin.'[29]

CHAPTER 8

Later developments in architecture

WE HAVE SEEN THAT THERE WERE two major waves of cultural influence in the nineteenth century, one beginning in the 1830s, the second in the 1880s, and that there was a very clear distinction between them. In architecture, however, development was steadier than in the other arts, and later styles grew out of earlier ones, rather than being in opposition to them. This was because the architectural profession was economically stable (there was a constant demand for buildings), and also because it continued to look to the past for inspiration long after other arts had ceased to do so. There is evidence of steadily growing interest in ancient Irish architecture, carried on by architects of the earlier generation, and taken up by their heirs. W. H. Lynn's most consciously Irish work, St Patrick's Church at 45 Jordanstown, was built in the 1860s. J. J. McCarthy designed his most Hiberno-Romanesque building, the Mortuary Chapel at Glasnevin, in the early 1870s. Nor 49 was such borrowing confined to native architects. It is interesting that several English architects working in Ireland also adopted details from Irish architecture. When E. W. Godwin (1833–86) built Dromore Castle, Co. Limerick, in 1868–70 102 for the Earl of Limerick, he crowned the composition with an Irish round tower (at least it is Irish in silhouette, though it has rather large openings round the top which are not at all Irish), a picturesque touch which looks slightly incongruous, but gives the composition an outline like that of the Rock of Cashel. He also used 103 Irish stepped battlements.

The architects who most consistently adopted an Irish style towards the end of the century were George Coppinger Ashlin (1837–1921) and James Franklin Fuller (1835–1924). Ashlin was a Gothic Revival architect a generation younger than McCarthy.[1] He was educated at Oscott, the Catholic college outside Birmingham, and articled to Edward Welby Pugin (1834–75), whose sister he married. He and Pugin were in partnership until 1870, and were among the leading ecclesiastical firms in Ireland at a time when there was a boom in church building. The style of the firm, and of Ashlin himself after the partnership broke up, was a mixture of French and English Gothic, but later Ashlin became interested in Irish models. As early as 1877 he did a design for a domestic chapel for A. Moore, Esq., of Moores- 98 fort, Co. Tipperary, which in many of its details is remarkably like Cormac's Chapel 97 at Cashel.[2] The blind arcading along the sides of the nave repeats precise details of surface decoration, and the chancel and chancel arch are also very like Cashel, though Ashlin has enlarged the carved heads in one of orders of the arch. His main departure is in the decoration of the transverse arches of the nave, which at Cashel are plain. It is characteristic of the period to multiply decorative elements, accurate in themselves, so that the result is quite unlike the original. The same is true of

96 J. F. Fuller: carving over the west door of the Church of Ireland church at Rathdaire, Co. Laois. See pp. 128–29.

97 Looking east in Cormac's Chapel on the Rock of Cashel, Co. Tipperary, of 1127–34, a key source of inspiration for the Hiberno-Romanesque Revival (see ills. 98, 106).

98 G. C. Ashlin: design for a chapel at Moores-fort, Co. Tipperary, 1877 (National Trust Archive) – one of the offspring of Cormac's Chapel.

the monument in Glasnevin Cemetery that Ashlin designed for Cardinal McCabe, 99–who died in 1885.[3] It is round-arched, with stubby columns and cushion capitals, 101 and is encrusted, inside and out, with ornament carved by C. W. Harrison and Sons. The decoration consists of chevron and rope mouldings, interlace, and masks on some of the capitals. The floor has symbols of the four Evangelists in mosaic, inspired by ancient manuscripts. The figure of the Cardinal, however, is guarded by some very Gothic-looking angels, and similar figures crown the roof of the structure. Just as the decoration is much more thickly encrusted than would have been usual on an ancient building, the plan, too, is different: as Lynn had done at Jordanstown (p. 66), Ashlin chose a cruciform plan and rounded apse. High 45 Victorian architects rarely found the original Irish models quite interesting enough.

99–101 G. C. Ashlin:
monument to Cardinal
McCabe, in Glasnevin
Cemetery, Dublin,
completed in 1887,
with carving by C. W.
Harrison and Sons and
a mosaic floor (here, the
symbol of St Luke).

102, 103 *Opposite:* E. W. Godwin's Dromore Castle, Co. Limerick, of 1868–70, and its prototype, the cathedral and round tower on the Rock of Cashel. Godwin also used a later Irish motif, stepped battlements, seen again in Ashlin's church design (*right*).

104 G. C. Ashlin: design for the O'Connell Memorial Church at Cahirciveen, Co. Kerry, *c.* 1884 (National Trust Archive).

The O'Connell Memorial Church at Cahirciveen, Co. Kerry, designed around 104 1884, is a much odder mixture. It is basically in a French Gothic idiom, with tall, slim lancets and a rounded and buttressed apse; but it is liberally supplied with secular-looking circular turrets, crowned with very steep conical caps, and they and the nave and aisle walls have stepped crenellations in the characteristically Irish style revived earlier by builders of romantic castles. All of this, according to *The Irish* 102 *Builder* of 1 July 1885, gave 'an Irish character to the composition'. (In fact it doesn't, though the design is a charming one.)

Ashlin's inaugural address as President of the Royal Institute of Architects of Ireland in 1901 was entitled 'The Possibility of the Revival of the Ancient Arts of Ireland and Their Adaptation to Modern Circumstances'.[4] He said that the examples of the revival seen up to then had been in minor things like sepulchral monuments, Celtic crosses and illuminated addresses. He felt that the Institute should take its proper place in the revival that was then going on, and fulfil the object for which it had been founded, the advancement of architecture in Ireland, developing a national style.

Ashlin and his later partner Thomas A. Coleman had a mainly Roman Catholic practice, whereas the other chief exponent of an Irish style, James Franklin Fuller, was appointed in 1862 District Architect to the Ecclesiastical Commissioners, responsible for building for the Church of Ireland. He came of a Co. Kerry family, and was inordinately proud of his lineage. His autobiography, published in 1916, contains a family tree, headed 'The Seize Quartiers of Thomas Harnett Fuller and also of his wife Fanny Diana Bland; being the Trente-Deux Quartiers of their only son James Franklin Fuller'.[5] He trained in England, and was in the office of Alfred Waterhouse during the designing of the Manchester Assizes, and subsequently with M. E. Hadfield after he parted from George Goldie. There is very little about his architecture in his book, and no indication why he should have built in Hiberno-Romanesque, yet there are several church designs by him in that style, dating from the 1880s and 1890s, such as Rathdaire, Co. Laois, and Clane and Carnalway, Co. Kildare. In its account of the Carnalway church, consecrated on 22 December 1891, *The Irish Builder* described Fuller as an authority on Hiberno-Romanesque.[6] St Michael and All Angels at Clane was consecrated on 29 September 1883. Of the style chosen the leaflet issued at the time had this to say:[7]

> Those who have studied Lord Dunraven's 'Notes on Irish Architecture', and have learned that we possess a national style of architecture capable of exquisite beauty, especially adapted to buildings of moderate size, will not be surprised that an Irishman, building in Ireland, adopted the style closely allied to the Norman, and which is technically known as Hiberno-Romanesque.

It goes on to say that the architect did not hesitate to depart from the original models where it seemed proper: he did not use leaning jambs; the plan is cruciform, which as we have seen was unusual in ancient buildings; and no woodwork survived to be copied. The most strikingly Irish feature about Clane is the decorative carving, especially on the crossing arches and capitals, all executed in Dublin. Other decorative work was commissioned from English firms and artists, a common practice at the time. The Irish elements were adapted from ancient sources, and Fuller had the advice of Margaret Stokes (see p. 24), who 'brought her profound knowledge of the subject to bear in many useful suggestions'.[8] Like Ashlin's Mooresfort, Clane has more than a suggestion of Cormac's Chapel at Cashel, especially on the eastern arch of the nave and in the linked windows of the east end. It is not as unified, however – possibly because in Mooresfort we see only the architect's original design, whereas Clane was the victim of donations from parishioners, and has Florentine vases, brass vases of Indian work, rather poor glass from Heaton, Butler and Bayne of London, sgraffito work by Heywood Sumner, and cloisonné work by Clement Heaton, none of it much in keeping with the style of the architecture and stone-carving.

105 J. F. Fuller: Church of Ireland church at Rathdaire, Co. Laois. The front – like that of the Honan Chapel – is adapted from that of St Cronan at Roscrea (ill. 118).

106 J. F. Fuller: St Michael and all Angels, Clane, Co. Kildare, 1883, looking past the crossing to the east end. Compare Cormac's Chapel, ill. 97.

Fuller and Ashlin were not the only architects of the period to turn to native precedents for their buildings. There were others, though none quite so consistent. Timothy Hevey (1845–78), an interesting product of the Pugin and Ashlin office with a practice in the north of Ireland, designed a church at Dunlewy, Co. Donegal   107 (1877), with a round tower as a belfry.[9] Its effectiveness as a composition is heightened by its being set in open country, with Errigal as a background. William Hague (d. 1900), a pupil of J. J. McCarthy, made the original designs for Letterkenny Cathedral, Co. Donegal, in about 1891,[10] though it was completed by his pupil Thomas McNamara ten years later. As a mixture it is odder, and considerably less attractive, than Ashlin's O'Connell Memorial Church. The basic design is conventional Gothic   104 Revival, with pointed openings and Decorated tracery, on which has been superimposed an encrustation of Irish detail, carved and painted. The ceiling of the crossing,   v for example, is a Gothic rib vault painted with Celtic interlace, and the crossing arch has carved scenes from the lives of St Adhamhnan (or St Eunan, after whom the cathedral is named) and St Columcille. It is a continuation of the same spirit which, forty years earlier, put harps, shamrocks and wolfhounds on the reredos   2 of the Catholic church at Kilcock, Co. Kildare.

An interesting sidelight on attitudes to Irish architecture is to be got from the various exhibitions which followed on the Great Exhibition of 1851. The earliest ones in Ireland were housed, like their model, in iron and glass palaces, but had some architectural exhibits of Irish interest. A model of Petrie's O'Connell Memorial was shown in Dublin in 1853, and there was an antiquities section with casts of high crosses, and of the chancel arch and east window of Tuam Cathedral.   43 It was later in the century, however, and for Irish displays abroad, that the exhibition buildings themselves began to reflect an interest in native architecture.

The World's Columbian Exposition at Chicago in 1893 had an 'Irish Industrial   108 Village' largely devoted to the manufacture, display and sale of Irish cottage indus-   109 tries, presided over by Lady Aberdeen (see below, pp. 147–48). The entrance was a reproduction of the north doorway of Cormac's Chapel, and beyond it was a copy of the cloister of Muckross Friary, with a tree in the centre, and a tomb,[11]

> bringing to our minds not only the thought of the beautiful, picturesque ruins from which this reproduction is copied, surrounded by its graves of the heroes of bygone days, but also of the exquisite scenery of the surrounding district of Killarney, its mountains, its lakes, its islands.

At the far side of the quadrangle there was a copy of Blarney Castle. The interior was reserved for living quarters for village workers, but a staircase permitted the visitor to climb to the top to 'kiss the magic stone' (the catalogue does not make it clear whether or not they had borrowed the real one), and to survey all Ireland – in the form of a relief map. The other buildings around the courtyard were single- and two-storeyed thatched cottages – one, Lady Aberdeen's, called Lyre-na-Grena (translated as 'The Sunny Nook'), copied from a building at Rushbrook, Co. Cork. The designer was Laurence McDonnell, 'the rising young Dublin architect'. The antiquarian interest was also represented by a copy of an ancient Irish cross, made by Colles of Kilkenny, and a display of photographs of Irish antiquities taken by Lord Dunraven, arranged and published by Margaret Stokes.

The Glasgow Exhibition of 1901 had an Irish Pavilion designed by Thomas Newenham Deane which was 'appropriately a rendering of the time honoured Irish

107 Timothy Hevey: Catholic church at Dunlewy, Co. Donegal, 1877.

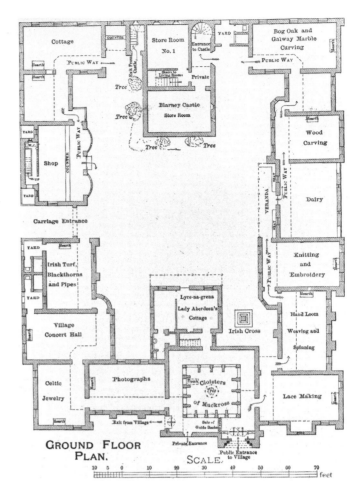

108, 109 View and plan of the Irish Industrial Village at the World's Columbian Exposition in Chicago, 1893, by Laurence McDonnell. See also pp. 147–48.

110 *Below:* the Irish Section in the Louisiana Purchase Exposition at St Louis, 1904. Cormac's Chapel is at the far left, the Drogheda gate and old Parliament House (by Pearce, 1729–39, with curved wings added by Gandon and others after 1780) in the foreground, and a simplified version of the domed Custom House (by Gandon, begun in 1781) behind.

GROUND FLOOR PLAN.

SCALE.

thatch'.[12] The same design was used again in the most spectacular of all the Irish exhibits abroad, at the Louisiana Purchase Exposition at St Louis in 1904,[13] immortalized by the song *Meet me in St Louis, Louis, Meet me at the Fair*. The principal entrance was a reproduction of St Lawrence's Gate at Drogheda, the Industrial Hall was a paraphrase of the Custom House in Dublin, the restaurant was an adaptation of the old Parliament House and the offices were in a recreation of the Council Chamber of the Royal Dublin Society. The archaeological exhibit was housed in a copy of Cormac's Chapel (the catalogue found it necessary to point out that 'this was not actually the real chapel where old King Cormac said his prayers'), in front of which was a copy of an ancient Irish cross. Sales of Irish industries took place in T. N. Deane's thatched cottage. The village also included a facsimile of the round tower of Clonmacnoise, part of Dublin Castle, a copy of Blarney Castle and the cottage of President McKinley's ancestors at Dervock, Co. Antrim. The buildings were constructed of expanded metal and plaster, though it was hoped that one or more of them could be of permanent materials. The designer was F. G. Hicks, an English architect settled in Dublin, and the exhibit was organized by the Department of Agriculture and Technical Instruction. It is curious, when one considers how lavish they were in the buildings, that they did not send Lane's collection of paintings because of the expense of insuring them (see pp. 107–08). It is yet another indication of the greater importance of arts and crafts at the time.

Another interesting feature of the St Louis exhibit was that it included Georgian buildings beside earlier ones, as representative of Irish architecture. Here, once again, we have the other strand of national feeling, which looked not to Ireland before the Norman invasion but to the period when Ireland had some legislative freedom from Britain, and when Dublin was a brilliant social and cultural centre. This interest was reinforced by a tendency common to England and Ireland (and the United States) at the end of the nineteenth century, to abandon medieval models and look instead to the eighteenth century. The Georgian Society, founded to survey and list Dublin Georgian architecture, held its inaugural meeting in 1908. Provost Mahaffy of Trinity College, speaking at that meeting, echoed the sentiments of Sir Samuel Ferguson half a century earlier (see p. 58) when he spoke of Dublin building of that period 'carried out mainly or altogether by Irish genius and Irish workmen'.[14] Just as Cormac's Chapel was the preferred model of the Hiberno-Romanesque Revival, James Gandon's Custom House in Dublin was favoured by the Georgian Revival. Aston Webb (1849–1930) and T. N. Deane drew on its river front for their Government Buildings in Upper Merrion Street, Dublin, begun in 1904. In 1912 R. M. Butler (1872–1943) referred to it for his competition-winning design for the front of the National University in Earlsfort Terrace. As late as 1923 Jones and Kelly won the competition for Cork City Hall with a design which distantly recalls, on the river Lee, the Liffey front of the Custom House.

The architect with the closest personal links with the Irish Renaissance was William Alphonsus Scott (1871–1921), once, in fact, described as architect by appointment to the Celtic Revival. He was the son of the architect Anthony Scott (1845–1919), who had worked in the Board of Works on historic monuments under T. N. Deane before setting up in practice on his own.[15] He travelled a great deal, notably in Italy, to look at buildings, and was a longstanding member of the Royal Society of Antiquaries of Ireland. The younger Scott studied at the Metropolitan

XIV Dun Emer Guild: symbol of St John, from a tapestry dossal designed by Evelyn Gleeson and Katherine MacCormack and made for the Honan Chapel *c.* 1917 (ill. XV). The design comes from the Book of Kells. See p. 164.

87

111
112

111, 112 W. A. Scott: St Enda's, Spiddal, Co. Galway, 1904–07, a free interpretation of the Hiberno-Romanesque style by the leading architect of the Celtic Revival. *The Irish Builder* in 1907 illustrated the building; the photograph of the west end shows Scott's distinctive use of rough and smooth masonry.

xv Altar furnishings in the Honan Chapel, Cork. The enamelled tabernacle by Oswald Reeves is flanked by candlesticks designed by W. A. Scott. (On the tabernacle door is the Lamb of God, and in the gable the Three Persons of the Trinity.) Behind hangs the tapestry dossal made by the Dun Emer Guild, and below is a frontal embroidered in the workshops of Barry Egan. See pp. 163–65.

School of Art in Dublin, and then in the office of Sir T. N. Deane and Son. After a spell in his father's office in Drogheda he went to London, where he worked for various other architects, and for the newly-created London County Council. He returned to Dublin in 1902, where his work soon began to attract attention, notably that of Edward Martyn and of the writer and critic Robert Elliott.[16] Martyn said that he had heard vague talk of there being a young architect somewhere in Ireland who was also an artist, and that this had seemed to him so wonderful a thing that he determined to seek him out. This he did, and recommended him to 'some friends in Spiddal' who wanted to build a parish church. Elliott was a journalist, an Englishman settled in Ireland, and was particularly interested in Catholic church art, and its reform. This gave him a great deal in common with Edward Martyn, whom he knew. He wrote about Scott's work in magazines like *The Leader* and *The Irish Rosary*, and in his rather laboured book *Art and Ireland* which appeared in 1906. In the same year Scott and Elliott went to Ravenna together, and to Constantinople to make a study of Byzantine basilicas in Turkey.

Edward Martyn's friend in Spiddal was Lord Killanin, and Scott designed for him a small stone parish church which became an important monument of the Celtic Revival. The foundation stone was laid in 1904, and bears an inscription in Irish which includes the words:[17]

> The Irish-Romanesque design of this church is by the architect William Scott, of Dublin; the outline and structure are after the model of the architecture of Eire in the days of saints and ollamhs [learned men] before the coming of the Gall [foreigner].

The parish priest, Father Conroy, said that it was the beginning of a new school

of Irish architecture, and the first attempt at a revival of the native architecture developed by the *Gael* before the coming of the *Gall*. It was consecrated in August 1907. Martyn said that Scott had 'entered into the project with enthusiasm which resulted in a little masterwork of design and charming appropriateness to the situation',[18] and that he had invented something like a modern Irish architecture inspired by old Irish buildings. St Enda's at Spiddal does indeed recall ancient Irish architecture. It is simple and sturdy, and has round arches and carved decoration with Hiberno-Romanesque associations. An alternative to the design which was built suggested a round rather than a square tower. Scott was very sparing of decoration, and looked to plainer and more primitive buildings than those which inspired Ashlin or Fuller, though oddly enough he too favoured a semicircular apse.

Another interesting design by Scott is the O'Growney Memorial Tomb, in the ecclesiastical graveyard at Maynooth, Co. Kildare.[19] Father Eugene O'Growney was among the founders of the Gaelic League, and wrote an Irish grammar which was much used. He died in California, but his body was later brought back to Ireland, and a tomb erected by the Gaelic League in recognition of his great services to the Gaelic Revival. Complete but for the doors in 1905, it is a very plain cell, with rubble walls of mixed stone and granite dressings, steeply roofed with slabs of granite. The openings are rectangular, each surmounted by a cross carved on a slab of stone. The whole effect is simple and rather austere, reminiscent of such solid and primitive Irish churches as Temple Benen on the Aran Island of Inishmore.

Scott is best known as the 'drunken genius' whom W. B. Yeats employed from around 1917 to supervise the restoration of Ballylee Castle, Co. Galway, an Irish medieval tower-house which the poet called Thoor Ballylee (Ballylee Tower), to avoid the suggestion of 'modern Gothic and a deer park'.[20] Yeats wrote of it:

I, the poet William Yeats,
With common sedge and broken slates
And smithy work from the Gort forge,
Restored this tower for my wife George;
And on my heirs I lay a curse
If they should alter for the worse,
From fashion or an empty mind,
What Raftery built and Scott designed.

Scott not only did schemes for the restoration of the fabric of the castle and attendant cottages but also designed furniture. 'This morning designs arrived from the drunken man of genius, Scott, for two beds', wrote Yeats to John Quinn on 23 July 1918; presumably one was the bed he later described in a letter to Sir Herbert Grierson as 'a great elm-wood bed made with great skill by a neighbourly carpenter, but designed by that late drunken man of genius Scott'. Scott also designed the wooden ceiling for Yeats's bedroom in the tower, and fireplaces for the building. An interesting feature of the whole scheme was the attitude of Yeats, and of his architect, to materials. The cottage attached to the tower was to be thatched, and stone for rebuilding came from old outhouses. They bought materials from a demolished mill, 'great beams and three inch planks and old paving stones',[21] and in his poem Yeats mentions 'common sedge and broken slate'. The work was done by local craftsmen – blacksmith, mason, carpenter. This use of local, and even used, materials, of country craftsmen and vernacular forms, a romantic feeling for native tradition which comes across very strongly in all Yeats wrote about Thoor Ballylee, is very similar to progressive English architecture of the period, and part of the Arts and Crafts movement. Scott's years in England had presumably exposed him to it. He certainly had a very strong feeling for materials and for workmanship. In a lecture to the Irish Architectural Association in October 1908 on Celtic architecture he dwelt on it particularly:[22]

> These early builders were well content to use the materials they found to hand. They did not, at least in early days, import stone easy to work, nor did they travel far for labour.
>
> In their massive buildings, their simple roofs, and their quiet but effective grouping of blocks of building, there is much to be admired and followed as a lead at the present time.
>
> Their ornament was simple, but not the less effective, and was all of a type easily done years after the completion of a building.

In 1907 Scott had designed, at Sheestown, Co. Kilkenny, for Captain Otway Cuffe, a member of the Gaelic League and enthusiastic Revivalist, a 'garden village' which with its thatch and lean-to roofs of Kilkenny flags made a particular feature of vernacular forms and local materials.[23] Earlier the bronze hinges for his O'Growney Memorial had been 'forged in an old-fashioned and honest manner in an Irish smithy by an Irish smith'.[24]

For his part, Yeats had lived as a boy and later as a young man in Bedford Park, a garden suburb on the western edge of London favoured by artists and writers,

114, 115 Thoor
Ballylee, Co. Galway,
restored by W. A. Scott
for W. B. Yeats. *Left*:
the tower-house and
cottages. *Right*: a room
in the tower-house with
timber ceiling by Scott.

which was an expression of the spirit that had sent architects like Norman Shaw
to make sketches of cottages in Kent and Sussex, or of small seventeenth-century
houses in country towns. Bedford Park aimed at a rural 'Old English' effect, with
trees and birds and pretty cottage gardens framing 'artistic' houses for people with
aesthetic leanings and little money. Yeats found the place idyllic, with thrushes and
blackbirds, perhaps even a nightingale. He planted pots on his balcony with 'sweet
peas, convolvulus, nasturtium and such like',[25] and filled the garden with sun-
flowers, apparently because he had always wanted a forest of the flowers, though
at the period they were specifically the emblem of aesthetes. Yeats of course moved
in Aesthetic and Arts and Crafts circles in London. Thoor Ballylee translates a good
deal of this into a less suburban Irish idiom, with a bit of Irish history thrown in
for good measure.

The O'Growney Memorial, St Enda's at Spiddal, and Thoor Ballylee are, for
a variety of reasons, Scott's best-known works. His output was, however, much
more extensive. It is sometimes difficult to disentangle, because he occasionally
worked in partnership with his father, and occasionally his father stepped in when
he was unable to work. He designed an agricultural college at Athenry, Co. Galway,
for the Department of Agriculture and Technical Instruction, a theological college
for the Galway Diocese, and a cathedral for the city of Galway which was, unfortunately, not built. Though he was closely involved with the Celtic Revival, working
for Yeats, for Edward Martyn (for whom he did some alterations at Tullira), for
the Gaelic Revivalist Otway Cuffe, and for the Gaelic League itself, he also seems

116, 117 James F.
McMullen: Honan
Chapel, University
College, Cork, 1916.
The carving (*above*, a
detail of the west door)
is by Henry Emery and
workmen from Cork
Technical School; the
strap hinges were
probably designed by
W. A. Scott.

118 St Cronan's at
Roscrea, Co.
Tipperary, the 12th-
century model for the
Honan Chapel façade
and that of Rathdaire
(ill. 105).

to have had a flourishing commercial practice. In addition to this, he was made Professor of Architecture in the National University in 1911. Scott's death at Cannes was announced by *The Times* in 1918, because it had confused him with another William Scott, ARIBA, Soane Medallist, author of *The Riviera* and *Rock Villages*. In fact he died three years later, in 1921, from pneumonia – developed, it was said, from a chill caught at the funeral of Archbishop Walsh.[26]

Apart from his architecture he had another connection with the Revival, through the Arts and Crafts movement. He designed fittings for the Cathedral of St Brendan at Loughrea, Co. Galway, a church for which so many of the leading artists and craftsmen worked that it constitutes a museum of the production of the period (see pp. 156–57). The building itself, designed by W. H. Byrne and completed in 1902, is in a fairly conventional Gothic Revival style. Scott also designed metalwork for the second major centre of patronage for Irish arts and crafts, the chapel of the Honan Student Hostel at University College, Cork, built in 1916 by a local architect, James F. McMullen. The design is not very distinguished, particularly in its use of round towers: the front, as at Rathdaire, is based on that of the ancient church of St Cronan at Roscrea, Co. Tipperary, and the interior draws to a certain extent on Cormac's Chapel. The furnishings of the Honan Chapel, like those of Loughrea, will be discussed in the next chapter (pp. 163–67).

116
133
134
xv
117
118

Hiberno-Romanesque was generally accepted as the style of the Celtic Revival, usually, it is true, for church building. There is one instance of its use for secular architecture, the Carnegie Library (now the Library and Museum), in Pery Square, 119 Limerick, designed by George Sheridan and built in 1906, but this is exceptional.[27] The Catholic church at Timoleague, Co. Cork, was designed in 1906 by M. A. 120 Hennessy of Cork, who seems to have won the commission in competition, since Scott did a competition design for the church.[28] The chief interest of Timoleague is the ruins of a Franciscan friary, so the architect decided to build the church in sympathy, 'Celtic Romanesque idealised so as to answer the requirements of a modern parish church'. *The Irish Builder* expected the effects of this choice of style to be as great as those of the Gothic Revival of seventy years earlier: Celtic Romanesque might well become a national style, 'enriched by the best of the past and by the skill and hope of the future'. Nothing of the sort was to happen. Leading church builders of the early twentieth century did adopt Hiberno-Romanesque from time to time. R. M. Butler used it for his church at Newport, Co. Mayo,

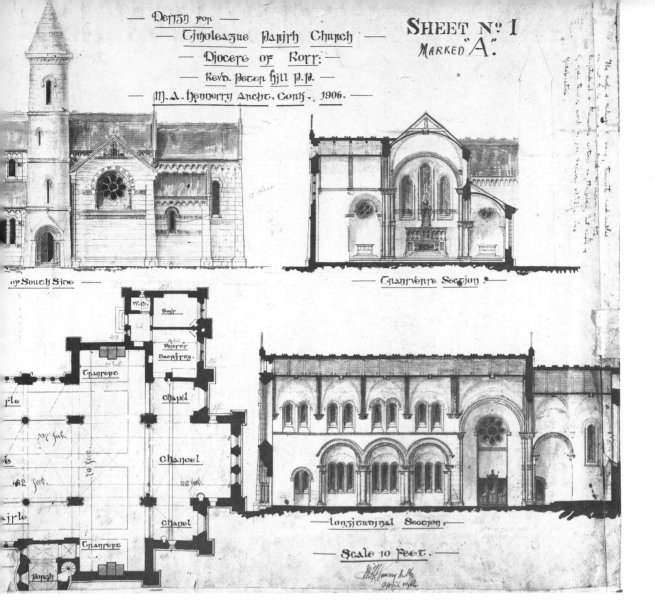

Design for
Timoleague Parish Church
Diocese of Ross:
Revd. Peter Hill P.P.
M. A. Hennessy Archt. Cork. 1906.

SHEET N? 1
MARKED "A."

of South Side

Transverse Section

W.C.

Transept

Chapel

Chancel

Chapel

Transept

Porch

Longitudinal Section

Scale 10 Feet.

120 M. A. Hennessy: architect's drawing for the Catholic church at Timoleague, Co. Cork, dated 1906 (National Trust Archive).

built after 1909, and, because he was familiar with the style, completed several of Scott's works. (He was also involved in the stained glass revival, as a friend of Sarah Purser and of Harry Clarke.)[29] J. J. Robinson chose Hiberno-Romanesque for his church at Lusk, Co. Dublin, which was hailed by Thomas MacGreevy in *The Irish Builder* for 21 March 1925 as 'another step on the road to re-mastering the art of building in the style known as Irish Romanesque'. As late as 1935 Ralph Byrne used it for the Church of the Four Masters in Donegal.

But Hiberno-Romanesque did not gain universal acceptance. This was partly because it was really only suitable for ecclesiastical work, and even in this it was rivalled by Byzantine and Italian Romanesque. Georgian styles were more popular for secular building, and were used a great deal, though they drew on English as much as on Irish models, and so constituted an Irish revival only to a limited extent. The hopes of those who had wished for a distinctly Irish style of architecture to emerge from the Celtic Revival were not realized, and the whole tendency to historicism was soon swallowed up by the Modern Movement.

CHAPTER 9

The Arts and Crafts movement

VICEREGAL SOCIETY IN DUBLIN, at the end of the nineteenth century and the beginning of the twentieth, was an area in which arts and crafts were important, largely because they gave the wives of Lords Lieutenant the chance to do active charitable work without getting involved in anything politically contentious. Lady Dudley was interested in the School of Art Needlework which was run by Lady Mayo. It was this school that embroidered the flag for an Irish Brigade in the 1914–18 war, which was returned to them when Kitchener refused to have the Irish as a separate unit.[1] Lady Londonderry's pet charity was Irish Industries, and Lady Cadogan was President of the Irish Industries Association. It was, not surprisingly, Ishbel Aberdeen who was the most active and involved of all. When she arrived in Ireland in 1886 she was already involved in preparations for an International Exhibition in Edinburgh, and she promptly organized an Irish section for it, with Irish girls spinning and lacemaking.[2] In the same year she inaugurated the Irish Industries Association with a very large garden party in the grounds of the Viceregal Lodge, at which the guests were requested to wear clothes of genuine Irish manufacture. The Association did a lot to encourage Irish cottage industries by providing classes and designs, and it also centralized and improved distribution, and attracted publicity. It prided itself on drawing together, on neutral ground, the various Irish factions – 'Roman Catholics, Episcopalians, Presbyterians, Methodists, Quakers, ... as well as Nationalists and Unionists of all sections'.[3]

Even after she and her husband had left Dublin Lady Aberdeen continued for a time as President of the Irish Industries Association, and took a leading part in the organization of the Irish exhibit at the World's Columbian Exposition in Chicago in 1893. As we have seen, this took the form of an Irish village, with Irish industries being carried out in the cottages. One had a turf fire with a potato pot hanging over it, and girls making lace and crocheting. Ellen Ahern, trained in the Presentation Convent at Youghal, Co. Cork, made needlepoint lace, Kate Kennedy appliqué work as it was practised round Carrickmacross, Co. Monaghan, and Mary Flynn crochet work. In the next cottage Bridget McGinley sat at her spinning wheel, preparing wool for Patrick Fagan, from Donegal, to weave. Nearby Maggie Dennehy, from Valencia Island, Co. Kerry, 'who talks real Irish', sat knitting. The dairy was staffed by three dairy-maids from the Munster Dairy School. The bog oak carving industry was also represented, 'both in the process of making and in its fully finished state, at the Darra-bochta store presided over by Miss Goggin'.[4] On the opening day 20,000 visitors paid their twenty-five cents entrance fee to the village, 'and were captivated by the sight of the rosy colleens, the sound of their musical brogue as they worked beside the turf fires in the cottages, dispensed buttermilk and butter in the model dairy, danced jigs and recited Irish verse in the village hall'.

108
109

121 The Dun Emer Press at work: Elizabeth Yeats is at the press; her assistants ink plates and, in the foreground, correct proofs. All wear flowing, unconventional pinafores. See pp. 158–60.

The village showed a profit of £50,000, the only other exhibits to do as well being the Cairo Street and the Ferris Wheel. Lady Aberdeen herself was indefatigable in her efforts to promote it. She arrived in Chicago before the opening,[5] and held a huge meeting at which one of her retinue, Josephine Sullivan, sang and played the harp. On the day of the American presidential visit she sent her husband chasing all over the Fair in an effort to press an Irish blackthorn stick on an obviously un-willing President Cleveland, and a Limerick lace handkerchief on his wife. She also took advantage of the Fair to establish more permanent markets for Irish industries. She got orders for Irish lace from Marshall Field of Chicago and from Baumharten, the New York decorators, and for Irish embroidered vestments from Cardinal Gib-bons, Archbishop Ireland and the Archbishop of New York.

The Celtic Revival affected costume in interesting and amusing ways. It was a period when people were attracted to fancy dress, and pageants were popular. These required people to invent Irish costume, based on what was known of medieval dress from illustrated sources and from ancient Irish literature. The widespread adoption of the kilt seems to have come from Eugene O'Curry's *Manners and Cus-toms of the Ancient Irish*, delivered as lectures to the Catholic University in the 1860s and published posthumously in 1873, with notes by W. K. O'Sullivan. O'Curry interpreted *leinidh*, a garment worn by the early Irish, as something reaching from the knees to the hips, which he concluded was a kilt, though others did not agree. Kilts worn at the time of the Revival were often saffron, a colour about which O'Sullivan, in a note, has this to say:[6]

> Garments dyed yellow with saffron are constantly spoken of by modern writers as characteristic of the Irish. There is no evidence, however, that saffron was at all known by the ancient Irish, and *lenas* and *inars* of a yellow colour are only mentioned two or three times in the principal ancient tales.

However, saffron must later have become a colour characteristic of the Irish, since Henry VIII issued a proclamation forbidding them to wear it. Kilts of saffron or green colour were worn by many people from 1900 onwards. Members of the Gaelic League, like William Gibson, later Lord Ashbourne, wore them, and so did patriots like Thomas MacDonagh and the Pearse brothers – Patrick with some reluc-tance, as he hadn't the figure for it.[7] A kilt was worn with a jacket, and a *brat* (like the Scottish plaid) fastened at the shoulder with a ring brooch of the 'Tara' variety, in copper, silver, or gold. The dress of women tended to be even more fanciful. Mary Colum, wife of the writer Padraic Colum, has left interesting descriptions of costumes worn by herself and her friends in the early years of the century.[8] A friend of hers used to appear at the Abbey Theatre in purple and gold, a torc on her forehead, her *brat* fastened by a 'Tara'-type brooch. She herself wore an Irish costume in blue-green, with a *brat* of the same colour decorated with embroidered designs out of the Book of Kells. Such costumes were made and exhibited by the Dun Emer Guild (see below) and won prizes.[9] In 1904 there were exhibits of Celtic 122 costumes at the third Arts and Crafts Exhibition in Dublin, made in Irish materials by Elizabeth Johnstone and Maeve Byrne.

Not everyone had the courage or the figure for such fancy dress, and the more conventional contented themselves with wearing materials of Irish manufacture, as Lady Aberdeen had advocated at her garden party in 1886. She herself appeared at the same party in a dress with Irish interlaced patterns embroidered on it – a

122 May Kerley,
needleworker at Dun
Emer, in an 'Irish'
costume made by the
Guild.

fairly early instance of 'Irish costume'.[10] Lady Fingall has an account of officiating at an Irish produce stall at a London exhibition, dressed in a coat and skirt of emerald green tweed, in which she waited upon Edward VII, to whom she sold a cigar, also of Irish manufacture. Irish tweed did not suit everyone. *Ireland's Own*, a rather conventional popular magazine, full of harps and shamrocks, and promising in one issue 'a famous battle every week', while urging its women readers to buy Irish whenever possible issued this warning: 'When one is getting on in years, and is perhaps short and stout, it is not the least use to advise Irish tweeds. They are too rough and bulky, and in few cases do they suit the elderly matron.'[11]

Quite apart from official interest in Irish arts and crafts it is clear that, except for Lane's Municipal Gallery, the aspect of Irish art that came closest to the literary and language revivals, and had most support from all the people concerned, was applied art. It had the active help of Edward Martyn, of Lady Gregory, and of W. B. Yeats, especially through the printing press run by his sister Elizabeth. It 121 was promoted by the Department of Agriculture and Technical Instruction, under Horace Plunkett and T. P. Gill and their successors, and it even aroused the enthusiasm of Douglas Hyde and the Gaelic League. The Earl of Mayo, who was a founder of the Irish Arts and Crafts Society, and also on one of the committees for the Municipal Gallery, drew these various strands together in a lecture to the National Literary Society in April 1905, entitled 'The Art Movement in Dublin'.[12] He said that the Gaelic League had arrived in time to prevent the snapping of the link that bound Ireland with her past, and he associated the Gaelic movement in a large measure with the progress of the art movement. He praised the admirable church

123, 124 Edmond
Johnson: silver sugar
sifter and sugar bowl.
The sifter (coll. Brian
de Breffny) is probably
one of the pair based on
the Charter Horn of the
Cavanaghs shown at
the first Arts and Crafts
Society Exhibition in
1896; the bowl
paraphrases the Ardagh
Chalice (ill. 10).

125 Hopkins and
Hopkins: silver 'Ardagh
Clasp', hallmarked 1912
(Ulster Museum,
Belfast). The two halves
of the buckle, which is
10.2 cm. (4 in.) wide,
are based on the motifs
below the handles of
the Ardagh Chalice.

126 Edmond Johnson:
silver mether, an
ornamented version of
the ancient Irish wood
or leather drinking cup,
1901 (coll. Brian de
Breffny).

windows of An Túr Gloine, the Dun Emer Industries (by then separate from the Dun Emer Guild: see p. 161), and metalwork from Five-Mile-Town, Co. Antrim, and in the most significant part of his talk he linked the craft revival and the gallery:

> These two movements – the movement for the education of the artist by the establishment of a Modern Art Gallery in Dublin, with its vitalising influence upon Irish painters and sculptors, and the movement for the better training of the craftworkers – are perhaps the most noteworthy indications of the direction which the stream of art tendency is taking in Ireland today.

Just as the earlier movement towards national feeling in Irish art was linked to the Gothic Revival in England, so the Celtic Revival was associated with the Arts and Crafts movement. The Arts and Crafts Society of Ireland was founded in 1894, with the objects of fostering artistic industries in Ireland, promoting artistic culture by means of lectures and the supply of designs, and holding exhibitions of Irish arts and crafts.[13] At the front of the first volume of the *Journal and Proceedings* is a poem by Walter Crane on William Morris. The Society held its first exhibition in Dublin in 1896. It was opened by the Lord Lieutenant, and inaugurated with an ode to Inisfail (Ireland), written by T. W. Rolleston and sung by a choir to music by Sir Arthur Sullivan.[14]

> Long ago, long, long ago,
> Through a mist of blood and tears,
> Through a thousand hapless years,
> See the golden vision glow!
> See thy craftsman's honoured hand
> Famed and loved in every land!
> Keen the eye and pure the thought,
> Holy was the hand that wrought,
> Long ago, long, long ago –
>   Ancient Inisfail!

> Children of the Gaelic race,
> Yours was once the gift divine –
> Masters of the magic line,
> Yours with tireless hand to trace
> Beauty through her winding ways.
> Cherish, then, the golden dream!
> Follow, then, the far off gleam!
> Guard your heritage of grace!
> Your faith, your patience, never fail,
> Your hope, your joy, your deathless dream,
>   Holy Inisfail!

XVI–XVIII Harry Clarke: windows in the Honan Chapel, Cork, *c.* 1916. See p. 163. *Left*, St Ita. She is presented by an angel with three jewels, representing the Trinity; below, she and her maids kneel in prayer to the Trinity. *Centre*, St Brendan. He is shown setting out in his coracle in search of the Islands of the Blessed; below, he meets Judas, chained to a rock in the middle of the ocean. *Right*, St Declan. Clarke illustrates the legend of St Declan and the bell and, below, his meeting with St Patrick.

The poem may be the usual mixture of history, religion, blood, and art, and lack polish in its rhymes, but it does express enthusiasm for Irish crafts. The revenue of the exhibition included fifteen shillings and ninepence for the sale of Mr Rolleston's ode.

In terms of the renewal of Irish crafts the 1896 exhibition itself does not seem to have been very exciting. William Hunt, invited to make an official report on the work shown, criticized the exhibitors for treating things pictorially rather than decoratively.[15] He found the workmanship in the furniture excellent, but thought the designs derivative. The gold and silversmiths' work was uninteresting, he said,

except for a case of pieces by Edmond Johnson.[16] This is odd, since a good deal of Johnson's work, the jewellery especially, is very like the kind of thing Waterhouse had begun to produce in the early 1840s, and which had been a feature of Irish exhibitions since that time. He showed adaptations of the 'Tara' and Cavan Brooches, a copy in silver and enamel of the Ardagh Chalice, a silver sugar basin 123 also based on the Chalice, with matching sugar tongs, and two silver muffineers adapted from the Charter Horn of the Kavanaghs. He also exhibited a casket of 124 Irish bog oak, embellished with silver and Irish stones, and 'copies of Antique Irish Sugar Bowls and Cream Jugs', the latter presumably from eighteenth-century rather than Early Christian models. The most interesting of his exhibits were methers, copies in silver of ancient Irish drinking cups. They are very elegant, and 126 must have been popular at the time, as quite a few survive. Johnson also made and sold a 'fibula brooch' which is almost indistinguishable in design from the one Waterhouse illustrated in his pamphlet of 1852. In fact the firm of Waterhouse also showed their fibula brooch at the 1896 exhibition, as well as the Brian Boroimhe Harp Brooch and the Tara Bracelet, which go back to 1852 at least. West, another leading maker of Celtic jewellery, was also still in active production. Relative new-comers to the field, Hopkins and Hopkins (established at 1 Lower Sackville Street by 1882), were to produce an illustrated catalogue of their gold and silver work about 1910 which also covers the full gamut of the designs made popular by Water-house: the 'Tara' Brooch in several sizes and materials, the fibula brooch, the Brian Boroimhe Harp Brooch, the Ogham (or Ballyspellan) Brooch, the Kilmainham Brooch, and many more. One of the most attractive of their designs was for the 'Ardagh Clasp', adapted from motifs on the Ardagh Chalice, and intended for 125 vestments or for ordinary wear.

The second exhibition of the Arts and Crafts Society, in 1899, was not much more exciting than the first. The report on it said that the attendance of the public was regrettably small 'and testified to the lack of cultivated interest in art industry which notoriously prevails in Ireland',[17] and the exhibition itself no doubt justified such apathy. The third exhibition, held in 1904, was quite a different matter. By then several key developments had taken place, partly as a result of a movement to persuade the Catholic Church to employ Irish artists, instead of importing glass from Munich and marble from Italy. An Túr Gloine and the Dun Emer Guild had been founded, and the decoration of Loughrea Cathedral was under way. In 1901 Edward Martyn had written in W. B. Yeats's magazine Samhain:[18]

> There are many movements now for the encouragement of Irish manufacture in all its branches, and for preventing the scandalous outpouring of Irish money into the pockets of Englishmen and other foreigners. Quite recently a movement has been started to turn the enormous demand for church art from the workshop of the foreign trades-man, and to get it supplied by the native Irish artist. It is impossible to calculate the sum of money that this will save the country. It will be enormous. Two such able and practical men as Mr Horace Plunkett and Mr T. P. Gill are so convinced of this that they have decided to form a school for the teaching of stained glass as a branch of the School of Art in Dublin, and have procured a teacher from probably the greatest master of the art in modern times.

XIX Harry Clarke: detail of a window in the Honan Chapel showing St Gobnet, patron saint of bees, loosing her hive against robbers of her sanctuary.

The classes began in 1903, under A. E. Child (d. 1939), a pupil of Christopher Whall. Martyn at the same time suggested to Sarah Purser that it would be a good idea to set up a studio where Child would be chief artist, and where others could work alongside him. This was the co-operative glass and mosaic works called *An Túr Gloine* (The Tower of Glass), in which most of the leading stained glass artists worked.[19] Sarah Purser (1848–1943) was herself a successful portrait painter; the daughter of a flour miller, she had studied painting in Dublin and the Académie Julian in Paris, and was noted for her support of Hugh Lane's gallery. 87

Both An Túr Gloine and the Dun Emer Guild (to which we shall return) were among those chosen to work at Loughrea Cathedral. It was Edward Martyn who persuaded successive Bishops of Clonfert, Dr Healy and Dr O'Dea, to employ Irish artists to decorate and furnish their cathedral, of which the fabric was complete in 1902.[20] His influence was no doubt reinforced by Father Jeremiah O'Donovan, who was curate at Loughrea from 1896 to 1902, and administrator from 1902 to 1904. In July 1901 he addressed the Union at the ecclesiastical college of Maynooth on the subject of Irish art, talking about the stained glass revival and the proposed work at Loughrea.[21] He told the young priests that since they controlled so much church decoration the art revival was in their hands. His lecture, printed in *The Irish Builder*, was headlined 'A Remarkable Pronouncement on Arts and Crafts in Ireland by an Irish Priest', and attracted a great deal of attention. Father O'Donovan was also connected with the Gaelic League, to which he gave the O'Growney Memorial Lecture in 1902.

The glass at Loughrea amounts to a gallery of specimens from An Túr Gloine. In the chancel and baptistery there is work by Child himself, rather watery arty-crafty, reminiscent of the Pre-Raphaelites. A little panel showing St Brendan, in the porch, is one of three pieces known to have been painted by Sarah Purser herself. There are some brilliant, jewel-like windows by Michael Healy (1873– 1941), and glass painted by Catherine O'Brien to Sarah Purser's design. The baptismal font, corbels and nave capitals, which have scenes from the life of St Brendan, IV 127 128 129

127, 128 Glass by An Túr Gloine in St Brendan's Cathedral at Loughrea, Co. Galway, 1904. *Left*: the infant John the Baptist, from the St Simeon window by Michael Healy. *Right*: the infant St Brendan, being handed a ship by an angel, from the window devoted to St Ita (Brendan's guardian), designed by Sarah Purser and painted by Catherine O'Brien.

129 Michael Shortall:
nave capital in
Loughrea Cathedral,
carved between 1902
and 1906.

were carved by Michael Shortall (d. 1951), who also worked for Edward Martyn on the baldacchino in his parish church at Laban, Co. Galway. W. A. Scott, brought in by Bishop O'Dea to replace W. H. Byrne as architect,[22] designed the metalwork and woodwork, and the side altars. There are some interesting wrought iron lamps in the nave, with inscriptions on them in Irish, all incorporating the word *solas* (light), and also huge brass candelabra. The benches for the congregation are very plain, but have fine little grotesque carvings on their ends. Most of the decorative work at Loughrea was done in the first twenty years of the century, though some of the stained glass is as late as the 1940s and 1950s.

A set of twenty-four embroidered banners for Loughrea, mostly depicting Irish VI–saints, was one of the first large commissions to come to the Dun Emer Guild.[23] XI They were worked in 1902–03 in silk and wool on linen, 'in the mediaeval style which was revived by William Morris', by Lily Yeats and her assistants, to designs by Jack Yeats and his wife Mary Cottenham Yeats. They are very fine, using dramatic colour and bold simplified shapes, similar to the 'Primitive' style which was also becoming popular in stained glass. They measure about 85 by 55 centimetres (33 by 21 inches), and cost four guineas each. The Guild also made several XII superb sets of embroidered vestments for the cathedral.

The Dun Emer Guild had been founded in 1902, when Evelyn Gleeson, Elizabeth Yeats and Lily Yeats set up craft studios in a house which they called Dun Emer, in Co. Dublin.

Evelyn Gleeson was born in England in 1855, the daughter of an Irish surgeon.[24] She grew up, she said, 'in an atmosphere charged with interest in industrial effort for the benefit of Ireland', as her father, who had become interested in the Lancashire textile mills, used the money he earned in England to start woollen mills in Athlone. She went to London to study art, and met disciples of William Morris, and members of the Arts and Crafts Society. She was told that she had an unusual gift for colour, and should take up carpet design, which she did, successfully. One of her teachers and also a close friend was Alexander Millar, a leading carpet designer and follower of Morris. She settled for a time in London, and seems to have been drawn into Irish society there: she was a member of the Irish Literary Society, and became friendly with the Yeats family.

The Yeats sisters, Susan Mary (1866–1949), known to everyone as Lily, and Elizabeth Corbet (1868–1940), known to her family as Lolly, but to everyone else as Elizabeth, were living at Bedford Park, where the family had settled in 1888 (see p. 141), and where Elizabeth kept house for her father, her brothers William and Jack, her sister and her ailing mother.[25] She trained as a teacher at a Bedford Park kindergarten, then taught art for five years at Chiswick High School, and lectured on painting and blackboard drawing at the London Froebel Institute.[26] She also did a certain amount of embroidery at home, and she was a talented painter in watercolours. During those London years she published several books on technique, including *Brushwork* (1896) and *Brushwork Studies of Flowers, Fruit and Animals* (1898).

Lily Yeats went, in 1888, as an assistant embroideress to May Morris, William Morris's daughter, who worked for her father's decorating firm. 'She likes it greatly; they make cushion covers and mantlepiece covers without end', wrote her brother William to Katharine Tynan on 4 December. She was paid thirteen shillings a week, with the prospect of more as she became experienced. By March 1889 she was training assistants for May Morris.

Evelyn Gleeson and the Yeats sisters had quite a lot in common, and when Evelyn had to leave London for the sake of her health, all three decided to return to Ireland and set up a group of workers in the arts. She borrowed £500 from a friend of hers, Dr Henry, and rented a house near the village of Dundrum, about ten kilometres (six miles) from Dublin. It was called Runnymede, a name which would not have done at all for an Irish craft centre, so it was renamed Dun Emer, 'the Fort of Emer', after the wife of the legendary hero Cuchulainn, who was famed for her skill in weaving and embroidery. In the autumn of 1902 the three women began work, recruiting local girls to train. They had advice from W. B. and Jack Yeats, and from T. P. Gill, and seem also to have got grants of money from the Department of Agriculture and Technical Instruction. They settled on three main crafts, based on their previous experience: embroidery, printing, and tapestry and rug-making. In addition to one of these each apprentice learnt painting and drawing from Elizabeth Yeats, and also had lessons in sewing, cooking, and the Irish language. The early pupils included Eileen Colum, sister of Padraic Colum, and Maire Walker, later celebrated as the Abbey actress Máire Ni Shiubhlaigh. The general effect was similar to Arts and Crafts circles in London, especially as regards dress.

130 John Butler Yeats:
Susan Mary (Lily) Yeats
(National Gallery of
Ireland).

Except for Evelyn Gleeson, who seems to have stuck to conventional Late Victorian
clothes, perhaps because she was older than the rest, they wore long, rather 121
'aesthetic'-looking pinafores, flowing loosely from square yokes or high waists.

The aim of Dun Emer, expressed in a prospectus produced in the second year
of their existence, was 'to find work for Irish hands in the making of beautiful
things'. As far as possible they used Irish materials – Irish paper for the books, Irish
linen to embroider on, Irish wool for the tapestry and carpets. Their designs, they
said, were of the spirit and tradition of the country.

> Things made of pure materials, worked by these Irish girls, must be more lasting and
> more valuable than machine made goods which only have a temporary purpose. All
> the things made at Dun Emer are beautiful in the sense that they are instinct with indivi-
> dual feeling and have cost thought and care.

That passage echoes the philosophy of Ruskin, passed on by Morris, about the freedom of the craftsman. It is interesting that Evelyn Gleeson owned, and obviously
read, since certain passages are marked, *Some Hints on Pattern Designing* (1899) by
William Morris. Her name is inscribed in Irish on the flyleaf. She seems to have
had more patriotic leanings than her partners.

FINTAIN.

Come here, fool; come here, I say.

BARACH.

(coming towards him but looking backward towards the door.) What is it?

FINTAIN.

There will be nobody in the houses. Come this way, come quickly; the ovens will be full we will put our hands into the ovens. (They go out.)

Here ends In The Seven Woods, written by William Butler Yeats, printed, upon paper made in Ireland, and published by Elizabeth Corbet Yeats at the Dun Emer Press, in the house of Evelyn Gleeson at Dundrum in the county of Dublin, Ireland, finished the sixteenth day of July, in the year of the big wind 1903.

131 Dun Emer Press: last page, with colophon, of W. B. Yeats's *In the Seven Woods*, 1903, the first book printed by the Press.

The printing began early in 1903, under the direction of Elizabeth Yeats, on a 121 small hand-press bought secondhand through an advertisement in an Irish paper. An eighteenth-century fount was chosen, 'not eccentric in form, or difficult to read', and the paper was made of linen rags without bleaching chemicals.[27] Elizabeth had learnt a little about typesetting in London under Emery Walker, and with the Women's Printing Society, but she knew nothing about press work, disliked machinery, and was even afraid of a sewing machine. The publicity makes a point of the fact that all the typesetting and printing was done by girls. The first book, *In the Seven Woods* by W. B. Yeats, appeared in August 1903. The press later 131 extended its efforts to prints and Christmas cards, which were hand-coloured. The editor of the books was W. B. Yeats, who chose what was to be produced. According to an announcement dating from about 1916, by which time the imprint was the Cuala Press, he selected works which had 'an intimate connection with the 132 literary movement in contemporary Ireland',[28] though he later admitted that he had had to annex Japan to Ireland in order to justify Ezra Pound's *Noh* plays.[29] He had an idea, which time was to bear out, that the books would be as characteristic of their time as the *Library of Ireland* had been to the Young Ireland generation.

The embroidery part of the enterprise was, naturally enough, under the direction of Lily Yeats. Designs were provided by Lily herself, Elizabeth Yeats, Jack and Mary Cottenham Yeats, and AE. As well as work for churches the studios produced embroidered articles for domestic use, such as cushion covers and portières. Several contemporary photographs show a portière with a rather Art Nouveau flavour, of seagulls embroidered on a white ground,[30] and another had peacocks embroidered on Galway flannel. Dun Emer embroidery work was frequently praised by contemporary critics, and *The Art Journal* in 1906 suggested that it was more distinctive than the printing. William does not seem to have shared this opinon: when one of her perennial crises caused Lily to appeal to him for money, he wrote to Lady Gregory on 8 February 1904 that he would need the opinion of someone like Charles Ricketts, Selwyn Image or Christopher Whall as to the quality of the embroidery. As late as 1937 he was relieved at Lily undertaking to do only what he directed, as he felt that this would keep her talent from being wasted.[31] Against the uncharitable thought that Elizabeth was of more practical use to him, since she printed his work and that of his friends, one should perhaps reflect that he often had to bail Lily out financially. He even set aside some of his Nobel Prize money in 1924 in case this should prove necessary.[32]

The tapestry and carpet weaving was under the direction of Evelyn Gleeson, and it, too, produced work for both ecclesiastical and domestic use. At the time when the Loughrea banners had just been completed the rug makers were working on VI– an altar carpet – described in the prospectus – for Donnybrook Church, Dublin, XI in green, with emblems from the Book of Kells, and a border of grapes and wheat.

It is clear from the accounts that Lily and Elizabeth were salaried assistants – technically at any rate, for each was very much in charge of her own area – at £125 a year. This is summed up in a letter from Evelyn Gleeson to T. W. Rolleston, written probably in 1904:[33]

> Up to the present the business has been entirely in my hands and I have provided funds for its working, which, however, I could not have afforded to do, if I had not been generously helped by a loan of £500 from my friend Dr Henry. This sum was placed at my disposal without conditions.

She said that she had been in touch with George Russell about the possibility of putting the business on a co-operative basis, as she couldn't possibly think of continuing it on the same lines as before, and that he had said that this could be done if the crafts were carried on independently as regards receipts and expenditure. If this were done the two Misses Yeats would become co-partners instead of salaried assistants. In 1904 Dun Emer split into two parts – the Dun Emer Guild run by Evelyn Gleeson, and Dun Emer Industries, run by the Yeats sisters.

Such was the situation when the third Arts and Crafts Exhibition opened in 1904. It was much smaller than the two previous ones had been, much more severity was exercised in the selection of exhibits, and only Irish work was shown. According to the *Journal* of the Society the exhibition showed for the first time 'something like a real upspringing of artistic feeling and endeavour among Irish craftsmen and craftswomen'.[34] It included printing and bookbinding from the Dun Emer Press, and rugs and carpets in Celtic designs by Evelyn Gleeson. There was also stained glass from An Túr Gloine. Some exhibits harked back to the middle of the previous century: the woodcarver Thomas Rogers, who, if he was the same man whose

POEMS AND TRANSLATIONS
BY JOHN M. SYNGE

CUALA PRESS
CHURCHTOWN
DUNDRUM
MCMIX

132 Cuala Press:
titlepage of Synge's
Poems and Translations,
1909. The lady and
tree vignette, by
Elenore Monsell, was
first used in 1907 on a
Dun Emer Press book.

work had been praised in the catalogue of the Dublin Exhibition of 1865 (see p. 84), must by now have been quite old, showed a bread trencher and potato bowl. They were exhibited, we are told, not for their design, but as examples of high technical accomplishment. The Committee of Selection considered that the bowl, with its design of naturalistic foliage, would have been better without the three feet carved in imitation of potatoes.

The Dun Emer partnership, as might have been expected with three such powerful personalities, had been an uneasy one from the beginning, and in 1908 the two groups separated completely. Evelyn Gleeson retained the name Dun Emer, while the Yeats sisters set up on their own at Rose Cottage, Churchtown, a few miles away, and called themselves Cuala Industries. According to the legal document laying down the terms of the split, the Dun Emer Press was to issue no further printed matter after the book then set up in type, and *A Broadside* for June 1908.[35] The printing press and type were to be delivered to Elizabeth Yeats (to become the Cuala 121 Press), and the sisters were to undertake not to carry on or promote, within the 132 County of Dublin for the next five years, the business of weaving carpets, rugs, or tapestries, artistic bookbinding, or artistic enamelling, or do any act whereby it might appear that the works carried out by the Dun Emer Guild Limited had been transferred to any place other than the residence of Evelyn Gleeson. Animosity is reflected in other places. An article on Dun Emer in *The Art Journal* for August 1906 speaks only of the work of Lily and Elizabeth, and later accounts of the history of Cuala tend to skate over the involvement of Evelyn Gleeson. One dating from the 1920s says that the press was founded by Miss E. C. Yeats 'together with Miss Gleeson', but that the latter 'retired from the partnership'.[36] Lily Yeats's tribute to her sister, published after her death in 1940, does not mention Miss Gleeson at all.

Evelyn Gleeson's account of the founding of Dun Emer, given in 1924, creates quite a different impression:[37]

> I was at that time very intimate with the Yeats family and full of sympathy with the girls. They were very anxious to go back to Ireland but could not, because of giving up their London employments and seeing nothing in prospect over here. We talked about Ireland and arts and crafts in which we were all interested. I had to go and leave my friends because London air was killing me. I thought how delightful to start a group of workers in the arts and keep my friends with me.

It is in any case certain that Lily and Elizabeth Yeats, having contributed little or no money, gained considerably from the split, in terms of stock and equipment.

The fourth Arts and Crafts Exhibition was held in 1910. By this time the Society had been reorganized, and a guild of craftsmen founded. It was called the Guild of Irish Art Workers, and its founding membership included A. E. Child, Evelyn Gleeson, Sarah Purser and Oswald Reeves. The latter was an enamel and metal-worker, brought in by the Department of Agriculture and Technical Instruction to teach in the School of Art, thus reinforcing the work already being done by the stained glass classes. From then on enamel, jewellery and metalwork became an important part of the Revival. Enamelling was added to the repertoire of Dun Emer some time before 1906, and Reeves himself made a very fine tabernacle door xv for the Honan Chapel.

The Honan Hostel Chapel in Cork, completed in 1916, fourteen years after Loughrea Cathedral, is the other great monument of Celtic Revival art.[38] Once again there is stained glass of a very high order, a lot of it by Harry Clarke (1889– xvi–1931), arguably the finest stained glass artist of the period.[39] Apparently the plan xix was to commission the work from An Túr Gloine, but when Sir John O'Connell, who was in charge of the scheme, saw Clarke's first window he entrusted more to him than he had originally intended. Clarke's windows are difficult to describe adequately, full of highly original and fantastic detail, exquisitely drawn in a style that recalls Beardsley, and both rich and brilliant in colour. Clarke, like the others, had studied under Child in the Dublin School of Art, but he also had the advantage of having grown up with access to a stained glass studio, since his father ran a firm of church decorators. Another very striking feature of the chapel is the mosaic floor, xx again full of brilliant colour and rich detail. It illustrates a Gaelic poem which sings the praises of God in all his works, and the canticle of the Three Children in the Fiery Furnace. The good stonecarving was done by Henry Emery and workmen 116 from the Cork Technical School, except for the figure of St Finn Barr over the west door, which is by Oliver Sheppard (1864–1941). W. A. Scott was involved, as at Loughrea, designing a set of altar plate – including a monstrance, candlesticks, 134 an altar lamp and an incense boat – which was executed by the silversmith Edmond 133 Johnson, and a grille for the porch made in wrought iron by J. and G. McLoughlin. XV

For the Honan Chapel the Dun Emer Guild made a cope and an antependium for the altar designed by Katherine MacCormack, Evelyn Gleeson's niece and principal assistant, and a dossal designed by the two women in collaboration. The dossal, XIV in red tapestry, has symbols of the four Evangelists as found in the Book of Kells XV and a rich border of Celtic ornament.[40] In the period after severing connections with the Yeats sisters, Dun Emer seems to have gone in a lot for embroidered vestments. There is very fine work by them at Loughrea and at St Michael's, Ballinasloe, in Co. Galway, and examples in quite a number of other churches and convents in Ireland and abroad, including the United States. In September 1921 Kitty Mac-Cormack wrote triumphantly to her aunt about Monsignor Rogers of the Church of St Patrick in San Francisco, a leading patron of Irish arts and crafts in the 1920s: 'We have just "landed" Monsignor Rogers . . . He has ordered a High Mass Gothic set, cloth of gold at £410–0–0 and Cope £150. I did him a terribly gorgeous design which simply knocked him flat!'[41] He asked for the vestments to be embroidered very finely, and planned to have them shown in the best jewellers in San Francisco, and written up in all the papers.

133, 134 W. A. Scott: silver incense boat and monstrance for the Honan Chapel, Cork, made by Edmond Johnson in 1916. The monstrance, 97 cm. (38 in.) high, has round the head a symbolic flight of doves, inspired by ancient manuscripts.

135 Detail of white
stole designed for the
Honan Chapel by Ethel
Josephine Scally and
made in the workshops
of Barry Egan, 1916.

Most of the vestments for the Honan Chapel were made in Cork, in the 135–
workshops of Barry Egan. Sir John O'Connell, in his book on the chapel, described 137
one set:[42]

The finest set of vestments consists of a cope, chasuble and dalmatics for High Mass,
made of cloth of gold, very richly embroidered with a subtle and delicate scheme of
interlaced work, was designed by one who united an extraordinary understanding for
the intricate beauty and mysterious charm of Celtic ornament with an exceptional
capacity for expressing its feeling both in line and colour; she has, unhappily, passed
away before she could see the working out of her exquisite designs. The orphreys of
the cope and of the chasuble and dalmatics have, let into their Celtic interlaced decora- XIII
tion, embroidered panels of the Evangelists, the wonder-working saints of Ireland and
of our Patron Saint of Cork, and they are completed by panels bearing the arms of
the Hostel.

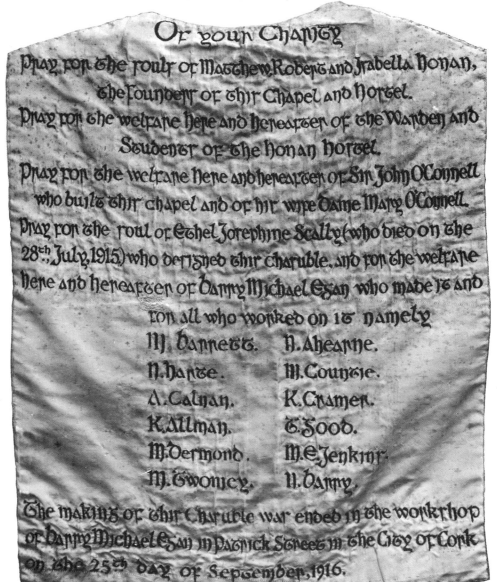

Of your Charity

Pray for the souls of Matthew, Robert and Isabella Honan, the founders of this Chapel and Hostel.

Pray for the welfare here and hereafter of the Warden and Students of the Honan Hostel.

Pray for the welfare here and hereafter of Sir John O'Connell who built this chapel and of his wife Dame Mary O'Connell.

Pray for the soul of Ethel Josephine Scally (who died on the 28th., July, 1915) who designed this chasuble, and for the welfare here and hereafter of Barry Michael Egan who made it and for all who worked on it namely

M. Barrett.	H. Ahearne.
H. Hante.	M. Countie.
A. Calnan.	K. Cramer.
K. Allman.	E. Hood.
M. Dermond.	M. E. Jenkins.
M. Gwomey.	H. Barry.

The making of this Chasuble was ended in the workshop of Barry Michael Egan in Patrick Street in the City of Cork on the 25th day of September, 1916.

136 Back of a chasuble from a mourning set of vestments designed for the Honan Chapel by Ethel Josephine Scally and made in the workshops of Barry Egan, 1916, embroidered in white and silver on black.

137 Embroidered inscription inside the chasuble of the cloth-of-gold Mass set (see ill. XIII), recording the death of its designer.

The designer in question was Ethel Josephine Scally, who died in 1915, and whose name, together with those of the embroidresses, is given on the inside of some of the vestments. 137

A lot of the work for the Honan Chapel was shown at the Arts and Crafts Society Exhibition in 1917, which was put on in collaboration with the Department of Agriculture and Technical Instruction. It was the fifth exhibition, and the catalogue is particularly magnificent. It is finely printed, on hand-made paper, and its cover 138 and the initial letter of the foreword were designed by Harry Clarke, who, besides being an outstanding stained glass maker, was a talented illustrator.

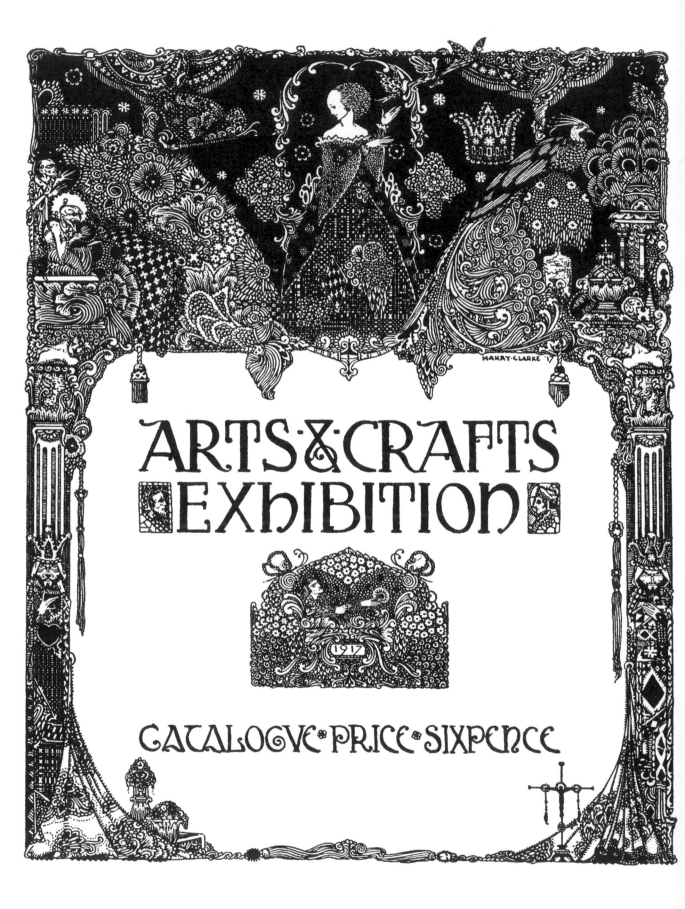

ARTS & CRAFTS EXHIBITION

1917

CATALOGUE · PRICE · SIXPENCE

The sixth exhibition was held in 1921. In his account of it in *The Studio* Thomas Bodkin said:[43]

> Hardly had the rain of bombs and bullets ceased to fall in the Dublin streets than it set about organising its sixth exhibition ... In spite of the fact that Irishmen – and Irishwomen – have been devoting more attention of late to the arts of war than to the arts of peace, this exhibition proves to be the best which the society has ever organised.

He felt that earlier exhibitions had had too much work based on Celtic ornament, and that a perverted patriotism had tended to poison taste. This exhibition, on the other hand, had little that suggested mere imitation of the Ardagh Chalice and the Book of Kells, and yet its displays – particularly the work of Harry Clarke, Oswald Reeves and the embroidery of the Cuala Workshop – conveyed an indefinable suggestion of being the product of the temperament peculiar to the Irish race.

At about this time there arrived on the scene a metalworker who was to become the best known of the Arts and Crafts movement, Mia Cranwill (1880–1972). She was probably born in Ireland, where her parents settled after leaving St Louis, Missouri. When she was about sixteen they moved to England, but she seems to have returned to Ireland by 1917, and her metalwork soon began to attract attention.[44] About 1925 she made a casket which was presented to the Irish Senate, intended to hold the original roll of the first Senate of the Irish Free State. The materials are gold, silver and enamel, on a copper foundation. A year later she was working on a tabernacle door for St Michael's at Ballinasloe,[45] which at that time was being filled by its administrator, Father Madden, with Irish craft work – glass, murals, and vestments, banners and carpets from Dun Emer. The tabernacle door is one of the finest products of the Revival. Of gold, silver and enamel, it represents Christ at Emmaus, the stylized figures close to, but not copied from, Irish work of the Early Christian period. There are panels of gold ornament like the chip-carving on the 'Tara' Brooch, and enamel bosses reminiscent of the Ardagh Chalice. The whole thing is distinctly Celtic in feeling, without being a copy or even a pastiche. Mia Cranwill did other ecclesiastical work, notably for Monsignor Rogers of San Francisco, for whom she made a clasp for an embroidered cope that he had commissioned from Dun Emer, a sanctuary lamp, candlesticks, and a magnificent monstrance, described in the memoirs of her friend Ella Young:[46]

xxiv

9

10

138 Harry Clarke: cover of the catalogue of the 1917 Arts and Crafts Exhibition.

139 Percy Metcalfe: 3d., 6d. and 2s. 6d. coins of the Irish Free State, from the set of designs that won an international competition in 1926 (see p. 175).

The work would take years, but she could put into it some of the passionate beauty of the Rising; something of the hard endurance of the men who died; something of the faith that renews itself through sorrow and loss in the Ireland that she loves. The monstrance was to be hand-wrought in gold, silver, and platinum, and enriched with tracery and enamels. Mia resolved to use, wherever possible, enamel à jour (enamel without a back). This would add to the labour and difficulty of the work, but would give when light touched it a jewelled effect as of stained glass.

This is rather high flown stuff, particularly when one considers that Mia Cranwill was born a Protestant and developed into an agnostic and that she was working for a Catholic church. She was, however, politically involved during the period of the black-and-tans (a particularly repressive soldiery sent to Ireland after the Rising of 1916, so called because of the mixed nature of their uniforms) and the Civil War, which would account for the mixture of patriotism and religion. She was also a member of the Theosophical Society, and a disciple of AE, and made jewellery based on themes from his book *The National Being* (1916).[47] One piece was a brooch designed to express the idea that 'actual forces are drawn from the Divine by the solidarity of a Nation'. It had a thick gold twist to represent 'the force of Nationhood reaching up through manifold individualities to the Divine, represented by the symbol of solar energy'.

The seventh, and last, Arts and Crafts Exhibition opened in 1925. In the preface to its catalogue Oswald Reeves felt it necessary to criticize a tendency towards the adoption of a distinctive national style derived from the Celtic tradition, 'in apparent unconsciousness of the dependence of National Style upon a determined vital striving on the part of a people to achieve in their actual lives their settled ideal of human dignity'. There was, by 1925, a reaction against the use of Celtic ornament, similar to the earlier reaction against harps and shamrocks, a feeling that you did not create an Irish art simply by reviving forms characteristic of Ireland in ancient times. Some craftsmen, like Mia Cranwill, or the stained glass workers, managed to assimilate Irish art of the Early Christian period to a wholly modern and personal vision, but lesser artists were inclined to lift designs wholesale from the Book of Kells, the 'Tara' Brooch, or ancient Irish crosses.

Two of the latest, and most exotic, flowerings of the Celtic Revival drew heavily on ancient manuscripts. One of these was *Leabhar na hAiseirighe*, or *The Book of* xxi *Resurrection*, commissioned by the Irish Government as a Republican memorial, to xxii celebrate independence. The artist was Art O'Murnaghan, who won the commission in competition in 1922. His work is exquisitely decorative, fine and intricately designed, and like that of Mia Cranwill is a mixture of Celtic ornament and eastern mysticism. Also like her work, it recalls Irish sources without being a copy. Unfortunately he died before the manuscript (now in the National Museum of Ireland) was completed.

The other late flower of the Celtic Revival was a chapel decorated by a Domini- xxv can nun, Sister Concepta Lynch (1874–1939).[48] She was the daughter of Thomas Lynch, a craftsman who specialized in those illuminated addresses so popular in the late nineteenth century, and was trained by him in that art. In 1920 she obtained permission to decorate an oratory in the grounds of her convent at Dunlaoghaire, Co. Dublin, and she continued to work on it until 1936. Using stencils, which she designed herself, she covered the entire walls, and to a lesser extent the ceiling, with

xx Detail of the mosaic floor of the Honan Chapel, Cork, c. 1915. See p. 163.

xxi, xxii (overleaf) Art O'Murnaghan: two pages from *The Book of Resurrection*, begun in 1922. *Left*, Men of the Coasts Page, commemorating the seafaring connections of the Rising, especially the deeds of Erskine Childers and Roger Casement. The rhythmic lines representing the movement of water and ships are oriental in feeling. *Right*, Treaty Page, commemorating the signing of the treaty with Britain in 1921. The design incorporates the map of Ireland, the pen of signature, and quotations relating to Irish history.

Τρεnna τυm τυδchaτορ ann τaρ
muim ζlan; ba ρlúaiζεδ ρεη
ζόιδιl co leiρ.   timnam braιn.

Strong the heroes who came there across
the clear sea; it was a hosting of men.—
Gaels in number.

Voyage of Bran.

MÓR AN
SNIOM DO
RONAD ANN .I.
TIONSAL AR TU
AT DE DANANN,
AGUS IS FADA DIOS
TIONSAL AGA DE
ANAM AN-EIR
INN DAEIS.
OIDE CLOINN
TUIREANN

NA CURU
ATA TAITH
MECHTA LA
FEINE
CUIR INDLISTEA ...
BEIM NAILLECH
NAD NERTAD
TUATHA ·
ISENCHUS MOR

Contracts which are
dissolved by the
FENI ......
Taking an Oath
which the
country
Does not
confirm

Initium Sanctu Evangelii secundum Joannem.

In principio erat Verbum, et Verbum erat apud Deum, et Deus erat Verbum. Hoc erat in principio apud Deum. Omnia per ipsum facta sunt: et sine ipso factum est nihil, quod factum est. In ipso vita erat, et vita erat lux hominum: et lux in tenebris lucet, et tenebrae eam non comprehenderunt. Fuit homo missus a Deo, cui nomen erat Joannes. Hic venit in testimonium, ut testimonium perhiberet de lumine, ut omnes crederent per illum. Non erat ille lux, sed ut testimonium perhiberet de lumine. Erat lux vera quae illuminat omnem hominem venientem in hunc mundum. In mundo erat, et mundus per ipsum factus est, et mundus eum non cognovit. In propria venit, et sui eum non receperunt. Quotquot autem receperunt eum, dedit eis potestatem filios Dei fieri, his qui credunt in nomine ejus: qui non ex sanguinibus neque ex voluntate carnis, neque ex voluntate viri, sed ex Deo nati sunt. (hic genuflectitur) Et Verbum caro factum est, et habitavit in nobis (et vidimus gloriam ejus, gloriam quasi Unigeniti a Patre), plenum gratiae et veritatis.

Celtic interlace and zoomorphic ornament. Much of this is a recognizable adaptation from such sources as the Book of Kells, but it is enlarged and repeated in such a way as to be quite unlike anything produced before, or indeed since: though the ornaments themselves are not very original the chapel is unique.

A symptom of the reaction against Celtic ornament can be found in the designs for the coinage of the Irish Free State. They were chosen by a Government Commission, set up in 1926 with W. B. Yeats as Chairman. He seems to have exercised considerable control over the final choice of design, which may account for the exclusion of 'outworn so-called national symbols, such as the shamrock, the sunburst and the round tower'.[49] The only vestiges of the conventional symbolism which were kept were the harp, which was to appear on the obverse of every coin, and the wolfhound, which was retained because it lent itself to noble and artistic treatment. An international competition was held, and the Commission laid down the imagery to be used, and sent pictures of harps (they recommended the Trinity College or the Dalway Harp), wolfhounds, and other animals to each competitor. In spite of a good deal of opposition from a public which would have preferred shamrocks, round towers, and the Treaty Stone of Limerick, the Commission had decided on a series of animals and birds as most suitable for a horse-riding, salmon-fishing, cattle-raising country. The half-crown had a horse, the florin a salmon, the shilling a bull, the sixpence a wolfhound, the threepence a hare, the penny a hen with chicks, the halfpenny a pig with piglets, and the farthing a snipe. Because some of the animals represented the national industry, agriculture, the designs were submitted to the Minister for Agriculture and his experts. The first bull had to go 'because it might have upset, considered as an ideal, the eugenics of the farmyard',[50] and the pig, too, was not considered suitable. There were Irish entrants in the competition – Oliver Sheppard and Albert Power, for example – but it was won by an Englishman, Percy Metcalfe; quite rightly, as he produced by far the most beautiful designs.

The competition, in a way, marked the end of an era, demonstrating that Ireland had not produced an artist of sufficient calibre to design her coinage, and that the symbols which had been used for over a hundred years to give an Irish stamp to arts and crafts were hackneyed and empty. The craft studios, An Túr Gloine, Dun Emer, Cuala, were still producing fine work in the 1920s, but the fervour which had held them together was fading, and the new state was too busy with matters of politics and economics to be much bothered with art.

XXIII   Altar card in the Honan Chapel, Cork, illuminated by Joseph Tierney and set in a frame of silver, silver gilt, enamel and crystals.

139

6

140 John Lavery: *Lady Lavery as Cathleen ni Houlihan*, 1923 (coll. Bank of Ireland, Dublin). See p. 179.

CHAPTER 10

Painting and sculpture after 1900

IF ARCHITECTURE AND THE APPLIED ARTS were closely bound up in various ways with the Irish Revival, painting and sculpture remained more aloof. This was partly because the tendency in European art in general was to move away from an interest in subject-matter towards considerations of form and treatment. The age of subject pictures with historic themes which could express nationalistic feelings had passed, and Irish art was not strong enough for a distinctly native style to take its place. The naïve tried to create an Irish School by resurrecting the old litany of titles from Irish history – St Patrick at Tara, incidents from the life of Brian Boroimhe, the battles of Clontarf, Aughrim, the Boyne, Fontenoy – but, except for the lowest level of popular imagery, there was no question of their being adopted.

The source of influence on Irish art had changed: whereas the earlier generation had looked to London, and occasionally to Rome, at the end of the century Irish artists went to Belgium and to France, and the dominant influences were Realism and Impressionism. Painters became more preoccupied with the medium than with the message, and even those who lived in Dublin, and were part of a society preoccupied with Irish culture and nationality, do not show it in their work. Walter Osborne (1859–1903) is a clear example of this.[1] Having studied in Antwerp and spent some time in Brittany, and in England with artists of the *plein air* school, he returned to settle in Dublin in the 1890s. He was part of the Dublin in which Yeats first became known, he knew Douglas Hyde, he visited Maud Gonne and George Moore, he went to soirées given by Lady Gregory. His family were Home Rulers. Yet there is nothing particularly Irish about his work, or anything to distinguish it in kind from that of his English, French, or Belgian contemporaries. He painted characteristically Irish scenes in the West of Ireland, of women in red petticoats, and men at horse-fairs, but clearly his interest in these subjects was similar to that which sent English painters to Newlyn in Cornwall and French painters to Pont Aven in Brittany – a search for unspoilt scenery and the rural life beloved of Realist painters. Osborne's best contemporary in landscape painting, Nathaniel Hone (1831–1917), is even less distinguishably Irish. His favourite subjects, lush pastures with cows, could be anywhere in England, Ireland, or northern France, and his manner is that of the Barbizon painters with whom he studied.

John Butler Yeats (1839–1922) had closer links with the Revival. He was lively and sociable, and knew many of the leading figures, either through personal association or through his children, and left us likenesses of many of them – writers, scholars, actors, artists, members of the language movement. Sarah Purser (see p. 156) counted among her sitters AE, T. P. Gill of the Department of Agriculture and Technical Instruction, Edward Martyn and Douglas Hyde.

92
93
87

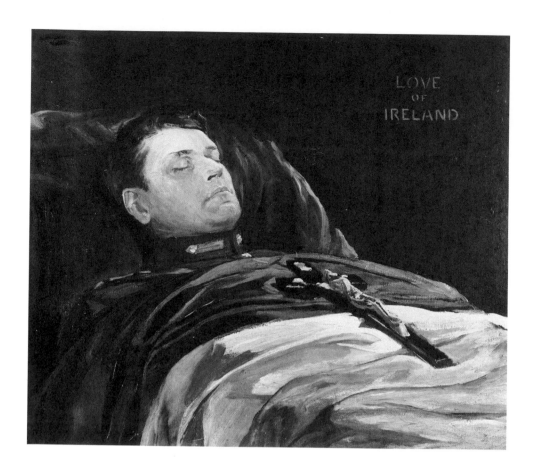

141 John Lavery: *Love of Ireland* – Michael Collins lying in state, 1922.

John Lavery (1856–1941) was older than Osborne, but as he lived much longer, and in his later work painted in an almost Fauve manner, he seems to belong to a later generation.[2] He was born in Belfast, but emigrated to Scotland when still quite young, and the larger part of his career was spent in Scotland, England and France. His interest in Ireland was aroused again when he settled in London during the First World War, and his sense of justice was offended by the behaviour of the black-and-tans. He reopened his affair with the country of his birth by painting a triptych of a Madonna and Child flanked by St Brigid and St Patrick, and presenting it to St Patrick's Church in Belfast where he had been baptized. To balance this, and show he was not a bigot, he presented 'the other side' with the sketch for a portrait group of the royal family which he had just painted. Then he began to paint portraits, choosing his sitters carefully from different sides of the religious and political fences. He painted Edward Carson, an Orangeman and Unionist, and John Redmond, a Nationalist and Home Ruler, on condition that their portraits would hang side by side in the Dublin Gallery. He painted the two Archbishops of Armagh, Cardinal Logue and Archbishop d'Arcy. At the time of the negotiation of the Treaty in 1921, he set himself to paint portraits of the signatories, including Michael Collins (1890–1922), 'a tall young Hercules with a pasty face, sparkling eyes, and a fascinating smile'. Lavery said that Collins was a patient sitter, but kept a gun in his overcoat pocket, from which he refused to be parted, and liked to sit facing the door. Lavery also painted *The Ratification of the Irish Treaty in the House of Lords, December, 1921* (National Gallery of Ireland). In 1922, after Collins had been assassinated, he painted his dead body, dressed in his soldier's uniform, a crucifix on 141 his breast, and covered by the Free State tricolour. He also painted his funeral in the Pro-Cathedral. (These two pictures are in the Hugh Lane Municipal Gallery, Dublin.) Lavery was, in a way, the chronicler of the emergence of the Free State. His most widely reproduced work was the picture of Erin or Cathleen ni Houlihan 140 with her harp (a portrait of his American wife, Hazel) for the Irish paper currency, painted in 1923.

Lavery's most distinguished contemporary was William Orpen (1878–1931), a 90 painter whose involvement with Irish nationalism was quite different. He was trained in the Dublin School of Art in the 1890s, at a period when the Revival was getting under way. Later he went to the Slade in London, where he was a contemporary of Augustus John, and for a time he shared a flat with Hugh Lane in Chelsea. Lane later commissioned him to complete the series of portraits left unfinished by John Butler Yeats. He came back and taught at the School of Art in Dublin in the years before the First World War, and was an occasional visitor to the Arts Club. His attitude to Ireland is difficult to assess. In his memoirs, *Stories of Old Ireland and Myself* (1924), he is very bitter about the treatment Dubliners meted out to benefactors like Hugh Lane, Horace Plunkett, and the trade unionist Jim Larkin; even Douglas Hyde, he said, 'who perhaps did more for Ireland than any living man', was nearly forgotten. Yet the book closes with a passage full of rather hackneyed Irish sentiment:

> A new era has come to the land. No longer is the shamrock put to shame by being trodden underfoot. No longer are men and women hanged 'for the wearing of the green.' Now the shamrock has its place in the sun, and long may it remain there, green and verdant.

It is possible, of course, that this passage is satirical. Between 1913 and 1916 Orpen painted three pictures with Irish themes which are very strange indeed in their attitude to Ireland and the Revival, and are certainly satirical. They are *Sowing New Seed in the Department of Agriculture and Technical Instruction for Ireland, A Western Wedding*, and *The Holy Well*.[3] All three are painted in a flat decorative manner, 142 influenced by Eastern art, and not unlike work of the period by Augustus John. Their treatment is rather shocking, though they are allegorical, and their precise symbolism is not easy to disentangle. *Sowing New Seed* was intended to symbolize the work of the Sinn Féin movement, and shows a young, almost naked girl pouring seed from her hand on to barren-looking ground. There are two babies in the picture, and a couple composed of a young woman and an old man. *A Western Wedding* caricatures the types and costumes of the West of Ireland, and the attitude of the people to religion, and is plainly anti-clerical. *The Holy Well* is a satire on the faith, or superstition, of Irish peasants, and its inclusion of nude figures in a context where, in the light of Irish society of the day, they seemed very much out of place, is deliberately startling. There are allusions in it to earlier works of art: the two figures in the middle, for instance, recall traditional representations of the Expulsion from the Garden of Eden.

Orpen's pupil Seán Keating (1889–1977), though stylistically very much influenced by him, is more straightforward in his attitude to Ireland. In the years from 1916 onwards he chronicled Ireland's military struggles, from the Rising

142 William Orpen:
The Holy Well, 1916
(National Gallery of
Ireland). The figure
standing on the left
above the well is
wearing traditional
West of Ireland clothes,
including the hide
slippers known as
pampooties (see p. 102).

through the black-and-tan period to the Civil War, in such pictures as *Men of the West* (Hugh Lane Municipal Gallery, Dublin), which shows some rather romanticized figures with guns and a tricolour, and *Men of the South*, a picture of an ambush 143 rather less glamorized.

Keating's older contemporary, Paul Henry (1876–1958), evolved a style of land- 144 scape with flat surfaces and simplified and stylized shapes, and painted a great deal in the West of Ireland. His pictures have a distinctly Irish flavour, and had many imitators among painters who wished to produce something characteristic of the country, without having to fall back on early Celtic art. As a result scenes that in Henry's hands had freshness and vigour degenerated eventually into insipid stereotypes.

143 Seán Keating: *Men of the South* (Crawford Municipal Art Gallery, Cork).

144 Paul Henry: *Connemara Landscape* (National Gallery of Ireland).

For most people the man who represents the Celtic Revival in painting is Jack B. Yeats, the poet's brother.[4] This is justified, even though it is partly because he *was* the poet's brother, and because his family were all closely bound up with the movement. There is nothing of the conventional Celtic atmosphere about his work, nor can it be described as Irish in style, since it is highly idiosyncratic, and its affinities are more with European Expressionism than with anything nearer home. However, his work draws on certain types and atmospheres powerfully evocative of Ireland, especially Dublin, and Sligo, with which he had family connections, and where he spent a lot of his boyhood. Thomas MacGreevy said of him that he 'filled a need that had become immediate in Ireland for the first time in three hundred years, the need of the people to feel that their own life was being expressed in art'.[5] This is misleading, in that it suggests popular success, which can't be said to have come to Jack Yeats until the 1950s at the earliest. On the other hand, he was one of the few painters of his time, perhaps even the only one, who managed to show a real and essential Ireland without sentiment or condescension or a striving for outlandish effect. Apart from these evocations of Irish life and atmosphere some of his pictures are directly political in content. A painting of about 1915, *Bachelor's Walk, in Memory* (coll. Lady Dunsany), commemorates the occasion in 1914 when the King's Own Scottish Borderers fired on a Dublin crowd, killing three people. *The Funeral of Harry Boland*, painted in 1922, shows the burial of a Republican opposed to the Treaty, who died during the Civil War of wounds sustained when he was being arrested. It is apparently the only record of the funeral, since all cameras were confiscated at the gate of the graveyard. For his family connections, his evocations of Irish life, and his political sympathies, Jack Yeats was clearly the most important Irish painter of the Revival.

83–85

145

145 Jack B. Yeats: *The Funeral of Harry Boland*, 1922 (Sligo County Library and Museum).

146 Monument to
Francis Prendergast,
killed in 1798, at
Monasterevan, Co.
Kildare, 1898.

147 Oliver Sheppard:
bronze figure on the
1798 Memorial,
Wexford, 1903.

Though there was no distinctively Irish style in sculpture any more than in painting, a connection with ideas of nationality is easier to isolate, because of the desire,
natural in an emerging nation, to put up monuments to national heroes. This had
already shown itself in the mid-nineteenth century, with the O'Connell Monument, 32
for example, but as far as more modern sculpture went it began with a series of
memorials to the men who had died in the rising of 1798. These began to appear
in the centenary year, 1898, though some were completed long after that. The choice 146
of sculptor and treatment was in the hands of local committees, which led to a wide
divergence in artistic quality, but some were very good. Two of the finest were
done by Oliver Sheppard, one for Enniscorthy, Co. Wexford, and one for Wexford 147
town which was unveiled in 1905. Sheppard also designed the memorial which
now commemorates the 1916 Rising, and stands in the General Post Office, Dublin. 149

148 Oliver Sheppard: bronze bust of James Clarence Mangan, from the monument in St Stephen's Green, Dublin, 1908.

It is a dramatic bronze of the dead Cuchulainn with a raven perched above him, 149 and is very suitable in subject and in treatment for its present purpose, though it was in fact made in 1911–12. Another work of Sheppard's is an indication of the links between this second wave of interest in Irish culture and nationality and the earlier one of the 1840s – a bust of the Young Ireland poet James Clarence Mangan 148 (see p. 24), which was unveiled in St Stephen's Green, Dublin, in 1909.[6] At the unveiling ceremony the Abbey actress Sara Allgood stood on a park bench and recited all fourteen verses of Mangan's poem 'The Nameless One'. Altogether, Sheppard may be said to have been the leading sculptor of the Revival, though he was not the leading Irish sculptor of the period: this distinction must go to his contemporary, John Hughes (1865–1941).[7] Hughes is connected with the Revival through the work he did for Loughrea Cathedral, a charming *Madonna and Child* in white marble, and a bronze altar relief, *The Man of Sorrows*, both begun about 1901. Both are quite un-Irish in style, and on the whole Hughes was like his friend the painter Walter Osborne in being more interested in art than in considerations of nationality. The major commission of his career was the Neo-Baroque monument to Queen Victoria (1903–06), which stood outside Leinster House in Dublin. It includes a figure of Erin leaning on her harp, holding a laurel wreath 150 for a dead Irish soldier, but it is not in any way an Irish patriotic monument.

149 Oliver Sheppard:
Cuchulainn, bronze,
made in 1911–12 and
later chosen as a
memorial to the dead
of 1916 and erected in
the General Post Office,
Dublin.

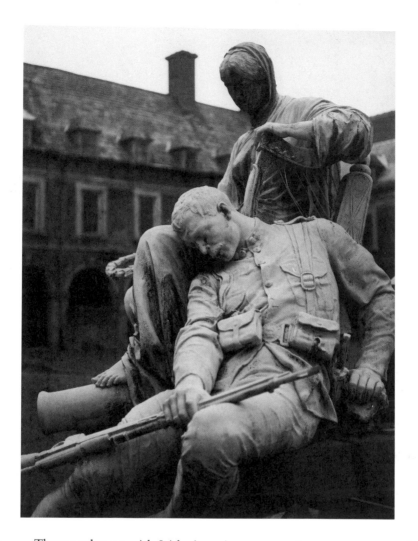

Three sculptors with Irish-American connections were among the leading pro-
ducers of statues of Irish heroes. Augustus Saint-Gaudens (1848–1907) was born in
Dublin, son of a French father and of an Irish mother, but his parents emigrated
to the United States six months after his birth. His Irish connection is very tenuous,
but he did one major national memorial, the figure of Charles Stewart Parnell for   151
the monument at the top of O'Connell Street, Dublin, completed about 1907. There
was opposition to the choice of Saint-Gaudens as sculptor, and a good deal of cam-
paigning in favour of Hughes,[8] but since a large part of the money was subscribed
in the United States, where Saint-Gaudens was well established, he won the
commission.

Andrew O'Connor (1874–1941) was born in the United States of Irish descent.[9]   33
Most of his career was spent there, and in France, but he lived in Ireland towards
the end of his life. Like Saint-Gaudens little of his work has any specifically Irish
connection; perhaps, indeed, only two pieces do: a standing figure of Daniel
O'Connell completed for the National Bank, Dublin, in 1932, and *Deirdre* (Hugh
Lane Municipal Gallery, Dublin), a woman's head, inscribed on the base with a
line from Synge, 'and it's cold your arms will be this night that were warm about
my neck so often'. O'Connor made a point of his Irish ancestry, and left a large

Within the image, inscribed text reads:

TO·THE·PROGRESS·OF·
IRELANDS·NATIONHOOD·
AND·WE·NEVER·SHALL·

ʒo ɼoɪɱbɪʒɪo Oɪa
eɪɼe oá claɪɲɲ

(base panels)
UL-STER CON-NACT LEIN-STER MUN-STER

151 Augustus Saint-Gaudens: bronze figure of Charles Stewart Parnell on his monument in Dublin, c. 1907.

collection of his work to the Municipal Gallery in Dublin. He was seen by a contemporary historian as possessing 'that strange celtic romanticism with its vivid dramatisation of life that is so typically Irish'. This may be so, but romanticism and drama are also qualities which distinguish Rodin, a major influence on O'Connor.

Jerome Connor (1876–1943), finally, was born in Co. Kerry, though his family emigrated to the United States when he was a boy.[10] He returned to settle in Ireland in 1925, and spent most of the rest of his life working on the *Lusitania* Memorial at Cobh. While he was still in the United States, however, he had done a full-length figure of the Irish hero Robert Emmet for the Smithsonian Institution, Washington. He was also in sympathy with the Irish Republican movement in the United States, and exhibited a portrait bust of Eamonn de Valera (untraced) at the Philadelphia Exhibition of Fine Arts in 1921.

In sculpture, as in painting, no distinctively Irish style emerges. The sculptors with whom we have been dealing do have stylistic qualities in common, but these they owe to certain influences prevalent at the time, especially those of French and Belgian Realist sculpture, and above all of Rodin. Any Irish qualities they share have more to do with birth and association, and with subject-matter, than with anything recognizable as an Irish style.

Conclusion

LOOKING BACK OVER THE PERIOD between 1830 and 1930 one is forced to the conclusion that there was no distinctively Irish style, and that the Irish Revival did not pass on a living tradition in art as it did in literature. While it is possible to follow threads of development from time to time, these become insignificant when seen against Irish art as a whole. Hugh Lane suggested, in the preface to the catalogue of his Guildhall Exhibition, that if one put the work of Irish painters together 'common race quantities' must emerge: certain artists and certain periods did produce work of a distinctly Irish character, some of it quite as good as anything created elsewhere in Europe, but these manifestations were isolated from each other, and not part of a continuous process or of a native impulse to seek expression in art. Expressions of Irish nationality in art were usually the result of external influences, from politicians or historians, for example, rather than from the artists themselves. Throughout the period the main common factors in the arts were an interest in Irish history, a growing sense of Irish identity, and a pride in Irish achievements of the past – concerns which were characteristic of Irish culture as a whole.

One of the continuous threads of development is to be found in architecture. It is possible to trace a consistent and growing interest in historic Irish architecture, from archaeologists like Petrie through successful High Victorian architects like Lynn and McCarthy to W. A. Scott and his adaptation of Hiberno-Romanesque to a free architectural style at the end of the century. This interest in medieval architecture (which only affected a small proportion of the total output, notably churches), was of course part of the medieval revival common to Europe as a whole. Irish medieval styles were often chosen for historical rather than aesthetic reasons – because they recalled Ireland's former greatness, and because they symbolized, for both the Catholic Church and the Church of Ireland, community with the Church of St Patrick, since each was anxious to prove its authenticity as the original Christian Church of Ireland. Similarly the revival of Georgian architecture was the result of pride in another great period of Irish achievement, the eighteenth century. It, too, coincided with a similar stylistic revival in England.

Attempts to create an Irish School in painting and sculpture were more sporadic, and were largely a question of subject-matter. They, too, were the result of external influences rather than a spontaneous expression of nationality on the part of artists. Thomas Davis attempted to create an Irish School by publishing a list of subjects from Irish history, and by recommending awards of prizes for historical works. His friend and adviser, Frederic Burton, seems to have been the only person at the time to have realized that this was not possible, that you could only have a national art when you had some great passion seeking expression through artists.

As late as the beginning of the twentieth century writers were suggesting that Irish art could be more Irish if only painters would produce pictures of the Battle of the Boyne or St Patrick preaching at Tara. Attempts to create an Irish School were also hampered by the fact that Ireland lacked confidence in her judgment in matters of art to such an extent that Irish artists were much more respected at home if they were successful abroad. That Maclise was among the artists chosen to decorate the Houses of Parliament at Westminster, or that Hogan was highly respected in Rome, was much more important to Irish opinion than their work itself.

At the end of the nineteenth century, when Irish literature was embarking on its most vigorous and distinctive period, leading painters and sculptors were not much interested in the expression of nationality in art. Their roots were in Europe rather than in Ireland. Lane, and those who helped him found the Municipal Gallery, hoped that the presence of a collection of modern art in Dublin would stimulate young artists and help to create a national school. Once again this was an attempt by intellectuals to force art into a particular mould, and in the absence of a general impulse to expression in art it did not succeed. In addition, any development of a national art in Ireland was overtaken by the Modern Movement, which did not take the expression of national feelings into account. It was much more interested in the question of style, and Irish art in the nineteenth and early twentieth centuries had not been sufficiently vigorous for there to be any possibility of a distinctive style common to a group of Irish artists.

There remains applied art. Some of the most interesting, and sometimes the most amusing, expressions of national sentiments were in this area. They were very varied, and emerged from all levels of society, though they were often ambiguous. The use of national emblems was a continuous phenomenon throughout the nineteenth century and into the twentieth. It is to be found in every form, from the coarse and vulgar to the decorative and charming. There is no doubt that it was often a sincere expression of patriotic feeling. But national emblems were also used for purely commercial reasons (in the souvenir trade, for example), or for political ones (as when Queen Victoria decreed in 1900 that Irish soldiers in the British Army were in future to wear shamrock on St Patrick's Day), so that they came to have about as much significance for Irish nationality as the tartan upholstery at Balmoral had for Scottish. The other means by which art objects took on an Irish character was by drawing on Early Christian designs, in metalwork, illumination and stone-carving. This is to be seen, for example, in the revival of Celtic jewellery, which does seem to have owed its considerable popularity to feelings which spread right through the Irish people, interest in history and pride in the past. Once again, however, this revival happened not because metalworkers wished to express themselves in this way, but because people's imaginations were fired by the historical associations of objects like the 'Tara' Brooch and the Ardagh Chalice. Also, the imitations, though often handsome, and certainly interesting, were only imitations, almost always mass-produced by mechanical means. Not one of them came near equalling the craftsmanship of the originals. Irish people took pride in the evidence of the skill of their ancestors as they could not in the skill of their contemporaries.

There was one aspect of applied art that produced fine and distinctive work which was Irish without drawing at all on shamrockery, and only in a creative way on Celtic ornament. This was the Arts and Crafts movement that formed part of the

Celtic Revival at the turn of the century. For once external influences – the political, literary, and language movements – coincided with talented artists who expressed the feeling of the times in what they made. Enough work was produced in stained glass, in metalwork, and in embroidery, of a high quality and with common characteristics, for it to be possible to say that we have here the expression in art of the Irish Renaissance. This revival lasted for some twenty-five years, from about 1902 until the third decade of the century. After that it began to fade away; though certain studios and individuals continued to work, the impulse which had once united them gradually disappeared.

The newly-founded state turned its attention to other things. There was, it is true, a Minister for Fine Arts in the second *Dáil* (Parliament), from August 1921 until January 1922, but the only mark he seems to have left is his name in the Dáil reports (he was George Noble, Count Plunkett), and he did not even join in the debates. Nor would he have had any real power, since the treaty which handed over authority to the Dáil was not ratified until January 1922. The Ministry was not maintained in succeeding Governments, and things degenerated to such an extent that Thomas Bodkin, in his *Report on the Arts in Ireland* (Dublin, 1949), could write:

> Measures which might have been taken effectively in 1922 to foster the Fine Arts and rehabilitate the art institutions of the country are no longer likely to prove sufficient. In the intervening twenty-seven years the resources of such institutions, and the status and power of those who administer them have been steadily curtailed rather than augmented. We have not merely failed to go forward in policies concerning the Arts, we have, in fact, regressed to arrive, many years ago, at a condition of apathy about them in which it had become justifiable to say of Ireland that no other country of Western Europe cared less, or gave less, for the cultivation of the Arts. It might almost have been assumed that any sense of responsibility for the welfare of Art had faded from our national tradition.

Bodkin went on to show that things were not so bad as they appeared, and that the Government had some sense of responsibility about the arts. In support of this he quoted from a speech made by the *Taoiseach* (Prime Minister) in the Dáil on 20 July 1949:

> While we are concentrating on our material advancement we should not, I think, neglect matters of the spirit. We should not neglect the effort to foster, and if necessary to create or recreate, a proper national tradition in art.

This sounds very well, if Irish statesmen had not been saying the same thing for the previous hundred years or more, with little result.

Anyone who shares the hopes and ambitions of the artists themselves can hardly avoid a sense of disappointment in the fact that a national style failed to materialize clearly. On the other hand, if one stands back from the period and looks at it dispassionately as part of a wider phenomenon, the Irish experience assumes a new dimension. For Ireland was by no means alone; elsewhere in Europe there were small nations struggling for independence and in that struggle trying to express their identity through the imagination. The progress of art in Norway, Sweden and Denmark offers remarkable parallels to that in Ireland: there too the mid-nineteenth century saw a vigorous interest in early medieval history (the period of the Vikings and the sagas); later in the century, this interest led to the adoption

XXIV Mia Cranwill: door of the tabernacle in St Michael's, Ballinasloe, Co. Galway, 1926. Of gold, silver and enamels, it shows Christ at Emmaus. See p. 169.

XXV Sister Concepta Lynch, O.P.: stencilled decoration in an oratory of the Dominican Convent at Dunlaoghaire, Co. Dublin, 1920–36. The seated figure bitten by a dragon, to the right of the window, is an enlargement of a tiny detail in the Book of Kells.

of relatively authentic stylistic features in decoration and building; and, to complete the parallel, there too the literary figures produced by the movement (Ibsen, Strindberg, Björnson) must be admitted to have outshone the painters and designers. Hungary is another example: there the search for a national style led one architect to design in the manner of Moorish India, on the theory that the Magyars originated in Asia, and another to find in Transylvanian villages living folk-art forms which could be used in church building and decoration. Finally, at the opposite end of Europe, the artists of Catalonia, whose past was if anything even more heterogeneous than that of Ireland, Scandinavia or Hungary, created a fantastically individual style made up of Moorish and Gothic elements plus an evocation of the Catalan mountain landscape. Here architecture was the dominant 'national' art form.

These parallels should enable us to see Ireland in a richer context and to assess it in different terms than those of simple success or failure. In a sense, all these nationalist movements failed, because national styles are not created by acts of will. In another, they all succeeded, for they expressed the nation's sense of continuity with its past. This in itself must exert its own influence on the future.

NOTES

Bold figures refer to page numbers in the text

IB = Irish Builder

1 Introduction

7 1 For the Irishman in nineteenth-century caricature see Lewis P. Curtis, *Apes and Angels*, Newton Abbot, Devon, 1971.

9 2 For an investigation of the shamrock see Nathaniel Colgan, 'The Shamrock in Literature: A Critical Chronology', *Journ. Roy. Soc. of Antiquaries of Ireland*, ser. 5, VI, 1896, 211–27, 349–61. My quotations are drawn from there: Campion, 216; Spenser, 218; Derricke, 217; Dinely, 349; Threlkeld, 354. See also John Ardagh, 'The Shamrock, A Bibliography', *Irish Book Lover*, XXI, Apr. 1933, 37–40.

10 3 On 'St Patrick's Blue' see John Vinycomb, 'Address on the Origin and Significance of our National Emblems', *Belfast Naturalists' Field Club, Report and Proceedings*, ser. 2, III, pt. 6, 1893, 502–17.

4 There are several examples in the National Museum in Dublin.

5 I, 1892, 95–97, and II, 1893, 207–11.

12 6 George Newenham Wright, *An Historical Guide to ... Dublin*, 2nd ed., London, 1825, 147–48. I am indebted to Edward McParland for this reference.

7 For the harp see Vinycomb, op. cit., 511.

8 Patrick Lynch and John Vaizey, *Guinness's Brewery in the Irish Economy, 1759–1876*, Cambridge, 1960. I owe this reference to Nicholas Sheaff.

13 9 The main sources on the wolfhound are Edmond Hogan S. J., *The Irish Wolfdog*, 1897, and Capt. Graham, *The Irish Wolfhound*, 1879, both reprinted from the original editions, Dublin, 1939.

10 For Gandon see C. P. Curran, *Dublin Decorative Plasterwork*, London 1967, 68–69 (Edward McParland drew my attention to this). For Barry see W. G. Strickland, *Dictionary of Irish Artists*, London and Dublin, 1913, I, 35. For Waldré see John Gilmartin, 'Vincent Waldré's Ceiling Paintings in Dublin Castle', *Apollo*, Jan. 1972, 42–47, and letter, Nov. 1972, 467.

2 The Antiquarians

17 1 See William Stokes, *The Life and Labours in Art and Archeology of George Petrie*, London, 1868, and also Strickland, op. cit.

2 *Reminiscences of my Irish Journey in 1849*, London, 1882, 63.

19 3 Quoted in Stokes, op. cit., 68.

20 4 Otway, *A Tour in Connaught*, Dublin, 1839, 182; this also gives a good idea of his attitude to religious difference. Otway is described in Stokes, op. cit., 67.

5 For a contemporary account of the historical department of the Ordnance Survey see Samuel Ferguson in *Dublin University Magazine*, XXIII, Apr. 1844. The suggestion that its disbandment was for political reasons is made in Rev. Patrick M.

MacSweeney, *A Group of Nation Builders, O'Donovan, O'Curry, Petrie*, Dublin, 1913, 50. This is useful too on O'Donovan and O'Curry, for details of whose careers see also the *Dictionary of National Biography*.

6 John Francis Maguire, *The Industrial Movement in Ireland as Illustrated by the National Exhibition of 1852*, Cork, 1853, 349.

22 7 Stokes, op. cit., 149 and 142.

8 Ibid., 142–43 and 150–51 for a summary of the round tower controversy.

9 Quoted ibid., 15.

23 10 See Strickland, op. cit., and also Oscar Wilde, 'Mr Henry O'Neill, Artist', *Saunders News-Letter*, 29 Dec. 1877.

11 See Jane M. MacFarlane, *Sir Frederic William Burton RHA*, dissertation for B.A. Mod. II, Trinity College, Dublin, 1976, and *Loan Collection of Works by Sir Frederick Burton RHA*, catalogue, National Gallery of Ireland, Dublin, 1900.

24 12 Lady Ferguson, *Sir Samuel Ferguson in the Ireland of his Day*, 2 vol., Edinburgh and London, 1896. My quotation is from I, 254.

13 For the Stokes family see William Stokes, *William Stokes, his Life and Works*, London, 1898.

14 See Terence de Vere White, *The Parents of Oscar Wilde*, London, 1967, and *The Letters of Oscar Wilde*, ed. Rupert Hart-Davis, London, 1962.

26 15 This and the following quotation are from *Tracts Relating to the Irish Archaeological Soc.*, I, Dublin, 1841, 5.

16 *Prospectus of the Irish Archaeological and Celtic Soc.*, Dublin, c. 1856, 1.

17 *Reminiscences*, op. cit., 41 and 48.

18 There are several interesting accounts of the trip: Martin Haverty, *The Aran Isles or A Report of the Excursion of the Ethnological Section of the British Association from Dublin to the Western Islands of Aran in September 1857*, Dublin, 1859; in Lady Ferguson, op. cit., I, 337–42; and in Stokes, *Petrie*, op. cit., 317 and 375–76, from which my quotations are taken.

3 Young Ireland

29 1 Charles Gavan Duffy, *Young Ireland*, London, 1896, I, 40. This book is the chief source of information on Davis, *The Nation* and *Young Ireland*; see also Gavan Duffy, *Thomas Davis: the memoirs of an Irish patriot, 1840–1846*, London, 1890, and M. J. MacManus (ed.), *Thomas Davis and Young Ireland*, Dublin, 1945.

2 *Young Ireland*, op. cit., 126.

30 3 Ibid., I, 70.

4 Stokes, *Petrie*, op. cit., 208.

5 Gavan Duffy, *Davis*, op. cit., 147.

6 Davis, 'Illustrations of Ireland', in his *Literary and Historical Essays*, Dublin, 1846, 168.

7 For Burton on national art see Gavan Duffy, *Young Ireland*, op. cit., I, 153 ff., and Cyril Barrett, 'Irish Nationalism and Art', *Studies*, LXIV, 256, Winter 1975. The latter paper is the source of many of the ideas on art and nationalism explored in this book.
8 Davis's ideas about art and nationality are discussed in 'National Art', printed in his *Essays*, op. cit., 155–56. The list of Irish subjects is included in the same collection, p. 169.
9 Ibid., 163.

31 10 For general information on the artists mentioned see Strickland, op. cit.; *Irish Art in the Nineteenth Century*, catalogue of an exhibition at the Crawford Municipal Art Gallery, Cork, 1971; and *Irish Portraits*, catalogue of an exhibition at the National Gallery, Dublin, 1969 and National Portrait Gallery, London, and Ulster Museum, Belfast, 1970
Catalogues of the Annual Exhibitions of the Royal Hibernian Academy were published in Dublin from 1826 onwards.

36 11 See Gavan Duffy, *Young Ireland*, op. cit., I, 126n.
12 *Irish Industrial Exhibition, 1853* (catalogue), ed. John Sproule, Dublin, 1854.

37 13 Ibid., Class xxx, The Fine Arts, p. 422. The section is signed 'E.P.' in Celtic script.
14 *Young Ireland*, op. cit., I, 89. Examples of the cards are illustrated.

38 15 Ibid., I, 126–27 and II, 153. See also Gavan Duffy, *Davis*, op. cit., 110.

39 16 *Young Ireland*, op. cit., I, 170–71.
17 Ibid., II, 151 ff.

4 Painting, sculpture and architecture

41 1 Augusta, Lady Gregory, *Seventy Years* (autobiography), ed. Colin Smythe, Gerrards Cross, Bucks., 1974, 141–42.
2 Ibid., 141.

44 3 For Maclise see James Dafforne, *Pictures by Daniel Maclise RA with Descriptions and a Biographical Sketch of the Painter*, London, [1872]; W. Justin O'Driscoll, *A Memoir of Daniel Maclise*, London, 1871; and *Daniel Maclise 1806–1870*, catalogue of an exhibition at the National Portrait Gallery, London and National Gallery of Ireland, Dublin, 1972.
4 The story of the Vatican casts – which are still in the Crawford School of Art at Cork – is told in *Dublin University Magazine*, XXIX, May 1847, 594, and in O'Driscoll, op. cit.
5 *Dublin University Magazine*, op. cit., 599.
6 See Dafforne, op. cit., 7, and *Dublin University Magazine*, XXXIV, 200, Aug. 1849.
7 *Dublin University Magazine*, XXIX, May 1847, 599.

45 8 *Davis*, op. cit., 147.
9 Algernon Graves, *The Royal Academy Exhibitors*, reprinted London, 1970, III, 156; also O'Driscoll, op. cit., 109.

46 10 1 June 1854, 166. I am indebted to Raymonde Martin for this reference.

11 Quoted in Terence de Vere White, *Tom Moore*, London, 1977, 74.

49 12 For the subject see O'Driscoll, op. cit., 81, n. 1. The poem is quoted from *Irish Melodies*, London, 1845, 61.
13 For Davis on Maclise and Moore see his *Essays*, op. cit., 165.
14 O'Driscoll, op. cit., 223. The painting has not been found, but there is a study for it in the British Museum, London.

50 15 On the unveiling *see IB*, 15 Oct. 1864, 205.
16 For a full account of the O'Connell Monument and the controversy surrounding it see Homan Potterton, *The O'Connell Monument*, Ballycotton, Co. Cork, 1973.
17 *IB*, 1 Oct. 1865, 238.

51 18 *IB*, 15 Aug. 1871, 213. On negotiations with Foley see *IB*, 1 Dec. 1865, 291; and see also *IB*, 1 Aug. 1871, 203, and 1 Oct., 256.

52 19 *Young Ireland*, op. cit., I, 153.

54 20 See 'Benmore' [John Clarke], *Memorials of John Hogan*, Glenarm, Co. Antrim, 1927. His return to Ireland was announced in *The Nation*, 22 Sept. 1849.

55 21 Lady Ferguson, op. cit., I, 163–64.
22 *Essays*, op. cit., 157.

56 23 1 Apr. 1859, 40.
24 For a discussion of the Castle Style see Alistair Rowan, 'Georgian Castles in Ireland', *Bull. of the Irish Georgian Soc.*, VII, 1964. For Johnston see Edward McParland, 'Francis Johnston, Architect', *Bull. of the Irish Georgian Soc.*, XII, 1969.
25 Craig, *Dublin 1660–1860*, London, 1952, 295.
26 Edward McParland, 'The Englishness of Irish Architecture?', *Cambridge Review*, XCV, 2220, May 1974.

58 27 S. Ferguson, 'Architecture in Ireland', *Dublin University Magazine*, XXIX, 174, June 1847, 693–94, 697.
28 Lady Ferguson, op. cit., I, 272.
29 See Maurice Craig's preface to the reprint of Mulvany's *Life of Gandon*, London, 1969.
30 Stokes (*Petrie*, op. cit., 134) and Lady Ferguson (op. cit., I, 43) both speak of Morrison's work for Petrie.
31 Jeanne Sheehy, 'Irish Railway Architecture', *Journ. of the Irish Railway Record Soc.*, XII, 68, Oct. 1975.

59 32 For a full account of the O'Connell Memorial and a copy of Petrie's report see Stokes, *Petrie*, op. cit., 369–72 and 433–37. For the monument as built see *A Guide Through Glasnevin Cemetery*, Dublin, 1879.

60 33 For O'Connell's training see *IB*, 1912, 532.
34 See Mark Tierney and John Cornforth, 'Glenstal Castle, Co. Limerick', *Country Life*, 3 Oct. 1974, 934–37.

61 35 For Adare see Caroline, Countess of Dunraven, *Memorials of Adare Manor*, printed for private circulation, Oxford, 1865. My quotations are taken from pp. 5 and 9.

62 36 G. N. Wright, *A Guide to the Lakes of Killarney*, London, 1822.

37 I am grateful to Paul Larmour for drawing Slane and Leighlinbridge to my attention.

38 *A Sermon Preached at the Consecration of Kinneigh Church, Diocese of Cork, on Wednesday August 27th, 1856*, Cork, 1856.

39 *IB*, 1 Oct. 1871, p. 249, in its report that 'an Irish antiquarian priest in the south of Ireland, several years ago, built a round tower at the end of his own garden'. The quotation that follows is from LeFanu, *Seventy Years of Irish Life*, London, 1893, 175–76. I am indebted to Maurice Craig for information on the tower, and for photographing it specially for me.

63 40 See Phoebe Stanton, *Pugin*, London, 1971. My quotation is from A. W. N. Pugin, *An Apology for the Revival of Christian Architecture*, London, 1843, 23, n. 13.

64 41 For Deane see *Public Works, Ireland, Reports*, 1875 ff., appendices on National Monuments and Ecclesiastical Ruins; also *St Mary's Cathedral, Tuam, Restoration*, a folder with illustrations of the church, *c.* 1861; and *IB*, 1 July 1864, 131, and 1 Feb. 1865, 34.

42 Quoted in Stokes, *Petrie*, op. cit., 408.

66 43 See Hugh Dixon, 'William Henry Lynn', *Bull. of the Irish Georgian Soc.*, XVII, nos. 1 and 2, 1974; and on Jordanstown Lt. Gen. W. J. Smythe, *A Notice of St Patrick's Church, Jordanstown*, printed for private distribution in 1868, from which my quotations are taken.

44 I am indebted to Roger Stalley for information about medieval Irish architecture.

67 45 See Jeanne Sheehy, *J. J. McCarthy and the Gothic Revival in Ireland*, Belfast, 1977. The dates given for McCarthy's churches are for the beginning of building.

46 Gavan Duffy, *Young Ireland*, op. cit., I, 127.

47 *Duffy's Irish Catholic Magazine*, Mar. 1847, 42.

69 48 Quotations from *A Guide Through Glasnevin Cemetery*, op. cit., 60 ff.

49 Smythe, op. cit., 11.

50 *The Complete Catholic Directory ... for 1845*, Dublin, 1845, 412.

5 Popular and applied arts

For help on this section I am very grateful to Douglas Bennett, Mary Boydell, Erinna George, The Knight of Glin and Elizabeth McCrum.

71 1 My information on Harrison comes from letters in the possession of his granddaughter, Mrs Sparrow.

2 See Ruth Edwards, *Patrick Pearse*, London, 1977.

72 3 According to O'Callaghan's obituary in *IB*, 16 Dec. 1905, 918.

76 4 *IB*, 1 Jan. 1889, 14.

5 On Burnet and Comerford see Curran, *Dublin Decorative Plasterwork*, op. cit., 89–90.

6 See J. Anthony Gaughan, *Listowel and its Vicinity*, Naas, Co. Kildare, 1973, 505.

78 7 For bog oak and the furniture industry see G. Bernard Hughes, 'Irish Bog-Wood Furniture', *Country Life*, CXLIX, May 1971, 3859; the *Illustrated Record and Descriptive Catalogue of the Dublin International Exhibition of 1865*, London, 1866, 303 ff.; and *The Art Journal*, 1865, 41 and 127. *Slater's Directory* is quoted in the mimeographed notes on the Irish furniture collection in the Ulster Museum, Belfast, compiled by Erinna George, October 1977.

79 8 The davenport and the scenes on it were identified by Erinna George: see her notes on Irish furniture, op. cit. For O'Connor's exhibits see *Royal Dublin Soc. Official Catalogue of the Exhibition of the Fine Arts and Ornamental Art*, Dublin, 1861, no. 210, and *Exhibition of Irish Arts and Manufactures*, Dublin, 1882, no. 1106.

9 *Irish Industrial Exhibition, 1853*, op. cit., Furniture, no. 24, and *Illustrated Record ... 1865*, op. cit., no. 715.

80 10 See the *Official Descriptive and Illustrated Catalogue of the Great Exhibition*, London, 1851, II, 735.

11 *Irish Industrial Exhibition, 1853*, op. cit., 408.

12 *Description of a Suite of Sculptured Decorative Furniture ... Designed and Executed by Arthur J. Jones, Son and Company*, Dublin, 1853.

84 13 At the 1853 exhibition Beakey's exhibit was no. 2 in the Furniture section. See also *IB*, 15 Feb. 1865, 49. My information on the O'Connell furniture comes from the Curator of the O'Connell house at Derrynane.

14 Maguire, *The Industrial Movement in Ireland ... 1852*, op. cit., 137.

15 *Art Journal*, 1865, 41 and 127.

16 For the Goggins see *Royal Dublin Soc. Official Catalogue*, 1861, op. cit., nos. 175, 181, 290.

85 17 *Ireland's Welcome to the Stranger*, London, 1847, 13.

18 White, *The Parents of Oscar Wilde*, op. cit., 114–15.

86 19 *Illustrated Record ... 1865*, op. cit., 303 ff.

20 *Irish Industrial Exhibition, 1853*, op. cit., 389.

87 21 Niamh Whitfield, 'The Finding of the Tara Brooch', *Journ. Roy. Soc. of Antiquaries of Ireland*, 104, 1974, 120 ff. According to Sir William Wilde it was 'found in the year 1850 with other objects in an oak box when excavating for the harbour wall at the mouth of the River Boyne, near Drogheda' (120–21).

22 Quoted in Waterhouse, *Ornamental Irish Antiquities*, Dublin, 1852, 1853, 10.

23 Ibid., 4.

90 24 See Derry O'Connell, *The Antique Pavement*, Dublin, 1975, 14–17.

25 See Mary Boydell, 'Made for Convivial

Clinking', *Country Life*, 26 Sept. 1974, 852–54, and 'A Versatile National Emblem', ibid., 23 May 1974, 1280–81.

26 See S. McCrum, *The Belleek Pottery*, Ulster Museum, Belfast, publication no. 188, n.d.

6 The Celtic Revival

95 1 In *The Academy of Literature*, 6 Sept. 1902, quoted in Synge's *Collected Prose*, ed. Alan Price, Oxford, 1966.

96 2 From Moore's autobiographical trilogy, *Hail and Farewell*, ed. Richard Cave, Gerrards Cross, Bucks., 1976, 77.

98 3 For Douglas Hyde and the Gaelic League see Dominic Daly, *The Young Douglas Hyde*, Dublin, 1974.

4 O'Growney Memorial Lecture, 29 Sept. 1902, published as Gaelic League Pamphlet no. 26, 2.

5 A Gaelic League Exhibition of Arts and Crafts was reviewed in *The Studio*, Nov. 1906, 165. The *Claidheamh Soluis* article is dated 30 Nov. 1904.

6 *Parliamentary Papers*, Royal Commission on University Education, Ireland, XXXII, 1902, 315–16.

101 7 See R. A. Anderson, *With Horace Plunkett in Ireland*, London, 1935.

102 8 Page L. Dickinson, *The Dublin of Yesterday*, London, 1929, 99.

9 See Anderson, op. cit., and Department of Agriculture and Technical Instruction for Ireland, *General Reports*, 1900 ff. (in *Parliamentary Papers*).

10 Lady Gregory, *Seventy Years*, op. cit., 414.

11 *IB*, 3 Dec. 1904, 822.

103 12 See Dickinson, op. cit., 49 ff. The verse is reproduced on p. 51.

13 *We Twa, Reminiscences of Lord and Lady Aberdeen*, 2 vol., London, 1925, and Marjorie Pentland (their daughter), *A Bonnie Fechter* (on Lady Aberdeen), London, 1952.

14 Quoted in Dickinson, op. cit., 14.

15 For the story of the clothes see Pentland, op. cit., 56.

104 16 See Lady Gregory, *Seventy Years*, op. cit., 340; W. B. Yeats, *Memoirs*, ed. Denis Donoghue, London, 1972, 117; and Elizabeth, Countess of Fingall, *Seventy Years Young*, London, 1937, 230.

17 *We Twa*, op. cit., II, 182.

18 Pentland, op. cit., 174.

105 19 Ibid., 153.

20 Ibid., 154.

21 *We Twa*, op. cit., II, 183.

22 *Seventy Years Young*, op. cit., 297.

7 Hugh Lane and the Gallery of Modern Art

Most of my quotations from newspapers and periodicals of the time come from a set of scrapbooks put together by someone in Hugh Lane's circle, and presented to the National Library of Ireland by Dr Thomas Bodkin. They cover, in a remarkably comprehensive manner, the Irish activities in which Lane was involved: there are five volumes on the Municipal Gallery, a further separate volume on the Gallery 1902–18, and one volume each on a new gallery for the Royal Hibernian Academy, the RHA Winter Exhibition in 1902–03, the Guildhall Exhibition, the Corot controversy, and the National Gallery 1914–15.

107 1 25 Jan. 1908.

2 For Lane see Lady Gregory, *Hugh Lane*, London, 1921. His meeting with Yeats at her house is described on pp. 30–31.

108 3 Ibid., 46 ff., also the catalogue, *Loan Collection of Pictures by Irish Artists*, London, 1904.

4 *Hugh Lane*, op. cit., 33–34.

5 Op. cit., x.

111 6 *Hugh Lane*, op. cit., 56 ff.

7 Ibid., 63.

8 Ibid., 69.

9 For an account of the collection see the *Catalogue* of the Municipal Gallery, Dublin, 1908, and the Municipal Gallery scrapbooks for the period of the opening, Jan. 1908.

112 10 *Daily Express*, 21 Nov. 1904, 6.

11 *Manchester Guardian*, 24 Jan. 1908.

12 *Claidheamh Soluis*, 25 Jan. 1908.

114 13 In general, see the Municipal Gallery scrapbooks, III, Nov. 1912. On the Corporation vote of money see *Irish Times*, 21 Jan. 1913, and *Northern Whig*, 24 Jan. 1913. On the Gaelic League collecting money, see letter to *Irish Times*, 13 Jan. 1913.

14 *The Times*, 15 July 1913. A copy of an advertising leaflet for the play is in the Municipal Gallery scrapbooks, IV, 67.

15 Quoted in *Cork Constitution*, 30 Nov. 1912, in an account of a meeting in the Mansion House, Dublin, part of a campaign for a new building.

16 Quoted from *Irish Times*, where it is dated 8 Jan. 1913. It was subsequently revised.

116 17 For Orpen's part in the affair see Dickinson, op. cit., 37. Dickinson was an architect in partnership with Orpen.

18 Letter to Ernest Boyd, 20 Jan. 1915, quoted in *Letters of W. B. Yeats*, ed. Allan Wade, London, 1954, 591.

19 For Yeats's comments on the various sites see his letters published in *Irish Times* and *Freeman's Journal*, 18 Mar. 1913 (*Letters*, op. cit., 579–80). On the Earlsfort Terrace site, see *Hugh Lane*, op. cit., 107.

20 On the Turkish Baths see Dickinson, op. cit., 37.

21 On the Stephen's Green site see *Hugh Lane*, op. cit., 105–07. Murphy's comments appeared in the *Evening Herald*, 3 Mar. 1913.

22 *Irish Times*, 18 Aug. 1913.

23 In *The Worker*, 2 Aug. 1913.

24 The Corporation's decision was announced in the Dublin *Evening Herald* on 19 Sept. 1913; Lane's letter appeared in the *Irish Times* on 20 Sept.

119 25 *Hugh Lane*, op. cit., 135–36.

26 Ibid., 221–29.

27 See ibid., 231–33, for a facsimile reproduction of the codicil. The subsequent negotiations and agitations are set out on pp. 234 ff. See also the Dublin Corporation's *Statement of the Claim for the Return of the Lane Pictures*, 1932, and Thomas Bodkin, *Hugh Lane and his Pictures*, Dublin, 1956.

28 *Parliamentary Papers, Report of a Committee Appointed to consider certain questions relating to 39 pictures bequeathed under the Will of the late Sir Hugh Lane*, 1926, XIII. Also *Debate in the House of Lords on 14 July 1924*, 1924, LVIII, 524–35.

29 Dickinson, op. cit., 39.

8 Later developments in architecture

121 1 For Ashlin see *IB*, Jan. 1921, 841.

2 Again, I am grateful to Roger Stalley for advice about the possible medieval sources of nineteenth-century architecture.

122 3 See *IB*, Feb. 1902, 1038–39.

128 4 Reported in *IB*, 30 Jan. 1902, 1018.

5 *Omniana, The Autobiography of an Irish Octogenarian*, London, 1916. Fuller's training and career are referred to on pp. 81, 87, 180 and 183.

6 *IB*, 1 Jan. 1892, 8.

7 [T. Cooke-Trench], *The Church of St Michael and All Angels, Clane*, Dublin, 1894, 12.

8 Ibid., 21.

131 9 I am indebted to Professor Alistair Rowan for details about Dunlewy Church, described in *Northwest Ulster* (Buildings of Ireland), Harmondsworth, 1979, 269.

10 See *IB*, 1 June 1891, 130.

11 *Guide to the Irish Industrial Village and Blarney Castle, World's Columbian Exposition, Chicago, 1893*, published by the Irish Village Book Store. The Village is described on pp. 11–15.

134 12 *IB*, 13 Feb. 1901, 622.

13 *IB*, 27 Feb. 1904, 108 and 111; also *Louisiana Purchase Exposition Through the Stereoscope*, St Louis, 1904.

14 *IB*, 7 Mar. 1908, 134.

15 For W. A. Scott see *IB*, 21 June 1913, 397, and 7 May 1921, 326 (obituary). For his father see ibid., 22 Feb. 1919, 95 (obituary).

137 16 For Scott and Martyn see Denis Gwynn, *Edward Martyn and the Irish Revival*, London, 1930, 218 ff. For Scott and Elliott's trip to Turkey see *IB*, 5 May 1906, 345.

17 *IB*, 16 July 1903, 1868; 25 Aug. 1906, 669; and 24 Aug. 1907, 577 and 582, where the inscription on the foundation stone is given.

138 18 Gwynn, op. cit., 218 ff.

19 *IB*, 8 Apr. 1905, 229.

139 20 For Thoor Ballylee see Yeats's letters to Olivia Shakespeare, Apr. (?) 1922 (*Letters*, op. cit., 680), to Quinn, 23 July 1918, which quotes the poem, later revised (ibid., 651–52), and to Grierson, 7 June 1922 (ibid., 686–87).

21 Letter to Quinn, loc. cit.

22 Published in *IB*, 28 Nov. 1908, 722–30.

23 See *IB*, 30 Nov. 1907 (ill. supplement), and Robert Elliott, *Art and Ireland*, Dublin, [1906], 138 n.

24 *IB*, 8 Apr. 1909, 229.

141 25 Letter to Katharine Tynan, 20 Apr. 1888 (*Letters*, op. cit., 68). For the Yeats family at Bedford Park see below, p. 158 and n. 25.

142 26 For the false and real obituaries see *The Builder*, 26 Apr. 1918, and *IB*, 7 May 1921, 326.

144 27 *IB*, 7 Apr. 1906 (supplement).

28 On Timoleague see *IB*, 20 Oct. 1906, 844, from which my quotations are taken, and 19 Oct. 1907, 189. For Scott's design see the supplement for 19 Oct. Some of Hennessy's designs are in the National Trust Archive.

145 29 For details about R. M. Butler I am grateful to his daughter, the Countess of Wicklow.

9 The Arts and Crafts movement

147 1 For Lady Dudley and Lady Londonderry see Lady Fingall, op. cit., 164 and 283; the story of the Irish Brigade flag is told on p. 348. For Lady Cadogan see the Aberdeens' *We Twa*, op. cit., II, 148.

2 Pentland, op. cit., 58.

3 *Guide to the Irish Industrial Village*, op. cit., 19.

4 Ibid., 12–13, for details of craft workers.

148 5 For the Aberdeens in Chicago see *We Twa*, op. cit., I, 308–32.

6 For the kilt question see L. O'Curry, *Manners and Customs of the Ancient Irish*, Dublin, 1873, III, 106, and I (O'Sullivan's notes), ccclxxviii–ix and cccciii, from which the quotation is taken.

7 Edwards, *Patrick Pearse*, op. cit., 46.

8 In her *Life and the Dream*, Dublin, 1966, 105–08.

9 Undated newspaper clipping on the *Oireachtas* of 1917, in the possession of the heirs of Evelyn Gleeson.

149 10 Photograph in Pentland, op. cit.

11 24 Mar. 1909, 13.

12 Reported in *Irish Independent*, 18 Apr. 1905, and *Irish Times* of the same day, from which the quotation that follows is taken.

152 13 See the Society's *Journal and Proceedings*, I, 1–4, Dublin, 1896–1906; also catalogues of its exhibitions: 1, 1895; 2, 1899; 3, 1904; 4, 1910; 5, 1917; 6, 1921 (untraced); and 7, 1925.

14 *Journal and Proceedings*, I, 1, 1896.

15 Ibid.

155 16 For Johnson's metalwork see the catalogue of the 1895 exhibition, no. 381, and also *The Artist*, Jan. 1896, 2 and 28–29.

17 *Journal and Proceedings*, I, 3, 1901.

18 'A Plea for a National Theatre in Ireland', *Samhain*, I, Oct. 1901, 14.

156 19 See *Twenty-Fifth Anniversary Celebration, An Túr Gloine* (pamphlet), Dublin, 1928.

20 See *IB*, 30 Jan. 1902, 1020.

21 For O'Donovan see Alan Denson, *John Hughes*, Kendal, 1969, 470. His address to

the Maynooth Union was published in *IB*, 18 July 1901, 809.

157 22 Thomas MacGreevy, 'St Brendan's Cathedral, Loughrea', *Capuchin Annual*, 1946.

23 Described in a prospectus issued in the second year of Dun Emer's existence, probably 1903. This and a great deal of other Dun Emer material can be found in a collection of Cuala Industries ephemera and photocopies in the Library of Trinity College, Dublin.

158 24 Most of my information about Evelyn Gleeson comes from her papers: for access to them, and for permission to quote from them, I am indebted to her heirs. The papers include several draft outlines of her career, from which I have taken the biographical details which follow.

25 For the Yeats family see *Jack B. Yeats and his Family*, catalogue of an exhibition at the Municipal Gallery of Modern Art, Dublin, 1972. Details about the early life of the family in Bedford Park may be found in W. B. Yeats's letters to Katharine Tynan: 12 Feb. (*Letters*, op. cit., 58), 14 Mar. (64), 4 Dec. (93) and 21 Dec. 1888 (99), and end Feb.–Mar. (115) and 21 Mar. 1889 (118).

26 Some details of the training of Elizabeth and Lily Yeats occur among Evelyn Gleeson's papers – probably information supplied in support of requests for grants.

160 27 For an account of the press see Lily Yeats, *Elizabeth Corbet Yeats*, Dublin, 1940. I quote from the Dun Emer prospectus of *c.* 1903.

28 In the collection of Cuala material in Trinity College Library.

29 Letter to Olivia Shakespeare, 9 Mar. 1933 (*Letters*, op. cit., 807).

161 30 It appears, for instance, in a photograph of Lily Yeats and her assistants, in Sligo County Museum.

31 Letters to Lady Gregory, 8 Feb. 1904 (*Letters*, op. cit., 430–31), and to Edith Shackleton Heald, 2 Aug. 1937 (ibid., 894–95).

32 Ibid., 13 Jan. 1924 (*Letters*, op. cit., 701–02).

33 The letter (Gleeson papers) is undated, but since it mentions that Dun Emer had been in existence for two years it probably dates from 1904.

34 *Journal and Proceedings*, I, 4, 1906.

162 35 Memorandum of Agreement, 6 July 1908 (Gleeson papers).

163 36 Undated offprint from the *Birmingham Post*, among the Cuala material in Trinity College Library.

37 In a letter to Mr [Stephen?] Gwynn, 26 July 1924 (Gleeson papers).

38 Sir John O'Connell, *The Honan Hostel Chapel, Cork*, Cork, 1916.

39 For Clarke at the Honan Chapel see James White and Michael Wynne, *Irish Stained Glass*, Dublin, 1963.

164 40 See the catalogue of the Arts and Crafts Society's fifth exhibition, 1917 (ante-

pendium, no. 3, dossal, no. 55, cope, no. 154), and also O'Connell, *Honan Chapel*, op. cit., 56.

41 Letter dated 22 Sept. 1921 (Gleeson papers).

165 42 Op. cit., 57.

169 43 Dec. 1921, 257.

44 For information about Mia Cranwill I am indebted to her niece by marriage, Mrs Julie Crompton, and it is also a pleasure to thank Anthony Wood for a great deal of help.

That she had returned to Ireland by 1917 is suggested by an announcement that she placed in the catalogue of the 1917 Arts and Crafts Society Exhibition, stating that she 'will shortly open a studio for the sale of handmade jewellery and enamels. Tuition given in various branches of applied art.' Her studio address is given as 14 Suffolk Street, Dublin.

45 I am grateful to Father O'Shea, Administrator, for allowing me to look at the inventory book for Ballinasloe. Mia Cranwill was at work on the door in 1926, and the cost was to be £250.

46 *Flowering Dusk*, New York, 1945, 185.

170 47 The jewellery is described in Ella Young, 'An Artist in Metal', *Dublin Magazine*, I, Jan. 1924, 548 ff., from which the quotations that follow are taken.

48 See *A Shrine of Celtic Art*, Dublin, [1977], with an introduction by Etienne Rynne.

175 49 From Yeats's introduction, 'What we did or tried to do', in *The Coinage of Saorstát Éireann*, Dublin, 1928, 5.

50 Ibid., 6.

10 Painting and sculpture after 1900

177 1 Jeanne Sheehy, *Walter Osborne*, Ballycotton, Co. Cork, 1974.

178 2 See Lavery's autobiography, *The Life of a Painter*, London, 1940, especially 199–224, from which my quotations are taken.

179 3 For the three paintings see *Irish Art 1900–1950*, catalogue of an exhibition at the Crawford Municipal Art Gallery, Cork, 1975–76, 55–58, from which the quotations about them are taken.

182 4 See Hilary Pyle, *Jack B. Yeats*, London, 1970. For the paintings see *Jack B. Yeats, Centenary Exhibition*, National Gallery of Ireland, Dublin, 1971, and Ulster Museum, Belfast, and New York, 1972.

5 MacGreevy, *Jack B. Yeats*, Dublin, 1945, 19.

184 6 For *Cuchulainn* see *Irish Art 1900–1950*, op. cit., 84; for *Mangan* see *Ireland's Own*, 26 May 1909, 5, and Lady Glenavy, *Today We Will Only Gossip*, London, 1964, 30.

7 See Alan Denson, *John Hughes*, Kendal, 1969.

186 8 Ibid., 70.

9 See Homan Potterton, *Andrew O'Connor*, Ballycotton, Co. Cork, 1974; the quotations that follow come from pp. 49 and 21.

187 10 M. Allen in *Capuchin Annual*, 1963–65.

BIBLIOGRAPHY

GENERAL

Dictionary of National Biography, Oxford, 1917 ff.

Bruce Arnold, *A Concise History of Irish Art*, London, 1977

Cyril Barrett, 'Irish Nationalism and Art', *Studies*, LXIV, 256, Winter 1975

J. C. Beckett, *A Short History of Ireland*, London, 1952

Thomas Bodkin, *Report on the Arts in Ireland*, Dublin, 1949

Brian de Breffny (ed.), *The Irish World*, London, 1977

Thomas Davis, *Literary and Historical Essays*, Dublin, 1846

Robert Elliott, *Art and Ireland*, Dublin, [1906]

Sir Samuel Ferguson, *The Cromlech on Howth*, London, 1861

Gaelic League, Pamphlets 1–29, Dublin, 1899–1902

Peter Harbison, *Guide to the National Monuments of Ireland*, Dublin, 1970

Peter Harbison, Homan Potterton and Jeanne Sheehy, *Irish Art and Architecture*, London, 1978

Martin Haverty, *The Aran Isles or A Report of the Excursion of the Ethnological Section of the British Association from Dublin to the Western Islands of Aran in September 1857*, Dublin, 1859

Françoise Henry, *Irish Art*, I (to 800) and II (800–1020), London, 1965, 1967

Joseph Lee, *The Modernisation of Irish Society 1848–1918*, Dublin, 1973

Proinsias MacCana, *Celtic Mythology*, London, 1970

Asenath Nicholson, *Ireland's Welcome to the Stranger*, London, 1847

Eugene O'Curry, *The Manners and Customs of the Ancient Irish*, ed. with an introduction by W. K. O'Sullivan, London, 1873

Gearoid O'Tuathaigh, *Ireland before the Famine*, Dublin, 1972

J. M. Synge, *Collected Works*, ed. Alan Price, London, 1966

BIOGRAPHICAL WORKS AND MONOGRAPHS, BY SUBJECT

Sir Charles Gavan Duffy, *Young Ireland*, London, 1896

Rev. Patrick M. MacSweeney, *A Group of Nation Builders, O'Donovan, O'Curry, Petrie*, Dublin, 1913

Earl and Countess of Aberdeen, *We Twa*, London, 1925

Marjorie Pentland, *A Bonnie Fechter ...* (on Lady Aberdeen), London, 1952

Jane M. MacFarlane, *Sir Frederic William Burton RHA*, dissertation for B.A. Mod. II, Trinity College, Dublin, 1976

Loan Collection of Works by Sir Frederic Burton RHA, National Gallery of Ireland, Dublin, 1900

Thomas Carlyle, *Reminiscences of my Irish Journey in 1849*, London, 1882

Mary Colum, *Life and the Dream*, Dublin, 1966

Sir Charles Gavan Duffy, *Thomas Davis: the memoirs of an Irish patriot, 1840–1846*, London, 1890

M. J. MacManus (ed.), *Thomas Davis and Young Ireland*, Dublin, 1945

Page L. Dickinson, *The Dublin of Yesterday*, London, 1929

Lady Ferguson, *Sir Samuel Ferguson in the Ireland of his Day*, Edinburgh and London, 1896

Elizabeth, Countess of Fingall, *Seventy Years Young*, London, 1937

J. F. Fuller, *Omniana, The Autobiography of an Irish Octogenarian*, London, 1916

Beatrice, Lady Glenavy, *Today We Will Only Gossip*, London, 1964

Augusta, Lady Gregory, *Seventy Years*, ed. Colin Smythe, Gerrards Cross, Bucks., 1974

'Benmore' [John Clarke], *Memorials of John Hogan*, Glenarm, Co. Antrim, 1927

Alan Denson, *John Hughes*, Kendal, 1969

Dominic Daly, *The Young Douglas Hyde*, Dublin, 1974

Thomas Bodkin, *Hugh Lane and his Pictures*, Dublin, 1956

Augusta, Lady Gregory, *Hugh Lane*, London, 1921

John Lavery, *The Life of a Painter*, London, 1940

W. R. LeFanu, *Seventy Years of Irish Life*, London, 1893

Daniel Maclise 1806–1870, catalogue of an exhibition at the National Portrait Gallery, London and National Gallery of Ireland, Dublin, 1972

James Dafforne, *Pictures by Daniel Maclise RA with Descriptions and a Biographical Sketch of the Painter*, London, [1872]

W. Justin O'Driscoll, *A Memoir of Daniel Maclise*, London, 1871

W. B. Stanford and R. B. McDowell, *Mahaffy*, London, 1971

Denis Gwynn, *Edward Martyn and the Irish Revival*, London, 1930

Jeanne Sheehy, *J. J. McCarthy and the Gothic Revival in Ireland*, Belfast, 1977

George Moore, *Hail and Farewell*, ed. Richard Cave, Gerrards Cross, Bucks., 1976

Andrew Nicholl 1804–1886, catalogue of an exhibition at the Ulster Museum, Belfast and National Gallery of Ireland, Dublin, 1973

Robert Dudley Edwards, *Daniel O'Connell and his World*, London, 1975

Homan Potterton, *Andrew O'Connor*, Ballycotton, Co. Cork, 1974

William Orpen, *Stories of Old Ireland and Myself*, London, 1924

Jeanne Sheehy, *Walter Osborne*, Ballycotton, Co. Cork, 1974

Ruth Dudley Edwards, *Patrick Pearse*, London, 1977

William Stokes, *The Life and Labours in Art and Archeology of George Petrie*, London, 1868

R. A. Anderson, *With Horace Plunkett in Ireland*, London, 1935

Phoebe Stanton, *Pugin*, London, 1971

William Stokes, *William Stokes, his Life and Work*, London, 1898

The Letters of Oscar Wilde, ed. Rupert Hart-Davis, London, 1962

Terence de Vere White, *The Parents of Oscar Wilde*, London, 1967

Jack B. Yeats, Centenary Exhibition, catalogue, National Gallery of Ireland, Dublin, 1971 and Ulster Museum, Belfast, and New York, 1972

Jack B. Yeats and his Family, catalogue of an exhibition at the Municipal Gallery of Modern Art, Dublin, 1972

Thomas MacGreevy, *Jack B. Yeats*, Dublin, 1945

Hilary Pyle, *Jack B. Yeats*, London, 1970

The Letters of W. B. Yeats, ed. Allan Wade, London, 1954

W. B. Yeats, *Memoirs*, ed. Denis Donoghue, London, 1972

Ella Young, *Flowering Dusk*, New York, 1945

APPLIED ARTS

Douglas Bennett, *Irish Silver*, Dublin, 1976
The Coinage of Saorstát Éireann, Dublin, 1928
C. P. Curran, *Dublin Decorative Plasterwork*, London, 1967
J. Anthony Gaughan, *Listowel and its Vicinity*, Naas, Co. Kildare, 1975
Hopkins and Hopkins, *Illustrated Catalogue*, rev. ed., Dublin, *c.* 1910
Arthur J. Jones, *Description of a Suite of Sculptured Decorative Furniture, illustrative of Irish History and Antiquities, manufactured of Irish Bog Yew*, Dublin, 1853
S. McCrum, *The Belleek Pottery*, Ulster Museum, Belfast, publication no. 188, n.d.
Derry O'Connell, *The Antique Pavement*, Dublin, 1975
Sir John O'Connell, *The Honan Hostel Chapel, Cork*, Cork, 1916
Etienne Rynne, 'The Revival of Irish Art in the 19th and early 20th Century', *Topic* (Washington and Jefferson College, Washington, Pa.), no. 24, Fall 1972
—*A Shrine of Celtic Art*, Dublin, [1977]
Twenty-Fifth Anniversary Celebration, An Túr Gloine, Dublin, 1928
Waterhouse and Co., *Ornamental Irish Antiquities*, Dublin 1852, 1853
George Waterhouse, *Antique Irish Brooches*, 1872
James White and Michael Wynne, *Irish Stained Glass*, Dublin, 1963
Michael Wynne, *Stained Glass in Ireland, principally Irish ... 1760–1963*, Ph.D. thesis, Trinity College, University of Dublin, 1976
—*Irish Stained Glass*, Dublin, 1977

ARCHITECTURE

Charles B. Bernard, *A Sermon Preached at the Consecration of Kinneigh Church, Diocese of Cork ...*, Cork, 1856
[T. Cooke-Trench], *The Church of St Michael and All Angels, Clane*, Dublin, 1894
Maurice Craig, *Dublin 1660–1860*, London, 1952
Caroline, Countess of Dunraven, *Memorials of Adare Manor*, printed for private circulation, Oxford, 1865
A Guide through Glasnevin Cemetery, Dublin, 1879
A. W. N. Pugin, *An Apology for the Revival of Christian Architecture*, London, 1843
Lt. Gen. W. J. Smythe, *A Notice of St Patrick's Church, Jordanstown*, printed for private distribution, 1868

PAINTING AND SCULPTURE

Algernon Graves, *The Royal Academy Exhibitors*, reprinted London, 1970
Rupert Gunnis, *Dictionary of British Sculptors 1660–1851*, rev. ed., London, n.d.
Homan Potterton, *The O'Connell Monument*, Ballycotton, Co. Cork, 1973
W. G. Strickland, *A Dictionary of Irish Artists*, London and Dublin, 1913

CATALOGUES, IN CHRONOLOGICAL ORDER

Royal Hibernian Academy, catalogues of annual exhibitions, Dublin, 1826 ff.
John Francis Maguire, *The Industrial Movement in Ireland as Illustrated by the National Exhibition of 1852*, Cork, 1853
Irish Industrial Exhibition, 1853, ed. John Sproule, Dublin, 1854
Royal Dublin Society Official Catalogue of the Exhibition of the Fine Arts and Ornamental Art, Dublin, 1861
Illustrated Record and Descriptive Catalogue of the Dublin Exhibition of 1865, London, 1866
Exhibition of Irish Arts and Manufactures, Dublin, 1882
A Guide to the Irish Industrial Village and Blarney Castle, Chicago, 1893
Arts and Crafts Society of Ireland, catalogues of exhibitions in 1895, 1899, 1904, 1910, 1917, [1921: untraced], 1925
Louisiana Purchase Exposition Through the Stereoscope, St Louis, 1904
Loan Collection of Pictures by Irish Artists, Guildhall, London, 1904
Municipal Gallery, Dublin, *Catalogue*, 1908
Irish Portraits 1660–1860, National Gallery of Ireland, Dublin, National Portrait Gallery, London, and Ulster Museum, Belfast, 1969–70
National Gallery of Ireland, Dublin, *Catalogue of Paintings*, 1971
Irish Art in the Nineteenth Century, Crawford Municipal Art Gallery, Cork, 1971
National Gallery of Ireland, Dublin, *Catalogue of Sculptures*, 1975
Irish Art 1900–1950, Crawford Municipal Art Gallery, Cork, 1975–76

152 'The End' – from *The Autobiography of the Rory O'More Branch of the Gaelic League*, Portarlington, Co. Laois, 1906.

ACKNOWLEDGMENTS

I would like to express my gratitude to the following people for their help: Martin Anglesea, Rev. Cyril Barrett S. J., Douglas Bennett, Nicola Gordon Bowe, Mary Boydell, Brian de Breffny, E. Byrne Costigan, Maurice Craig, Anne Crookshank, Roseanne Dunne, Gifford Charles-Edwards, Thomas Charles-Edwards, Rev. Wyn Evans, Aloys Fleischmann, The Knight of Glin, Erinna George, William Garner, Rev. Joseph Hurley S. J., Patrick Kelly, Emily Lane, Paul Larmour, Jeremy Maas, Robert McCarthy, Elizabeth McCrum, Edward McParland, Raymonde Martin, Rory O'Donnell, William O'Donnell, Rev. Diarmuid O'Leary S. J., Homan Potterton, Mairead Reynolds, Alistair Rowan, Nicholas Sheaff, Oliver Snoddy, Roger Stalley, Ann Stewart, John Tehan, Clare Tilbury, the Countess of Wicklow, Anthony Woods, and Michael Wynne. Also to the Administrators and Sacristans of the Cathedral of Clonfert, and the Church of St Michael, Ballinasloe; the staff of the Ulster Museum, Belfast; in Dublin the staff, Librarian and Library staff of the National Gallery of Ireland, the staff of the National Library of Ireland, the Director and staff of the National Trust Archive, and the Librarian and staff of the Royal Irish Academy Library; and the staff of the Library, Prints and Drawings Department and Metalwork Department, in particular Shirley Bury, of the Victoria and Albert Museum, London. Special thanks go to all of those friends, colleagues and relations who have put up with so much.

J. S.

For illustrations other than those by George Mott, or for permitting him to photograph objects in their collections, the author, photographer and publishers are grateful to the owners mentioned in the text and captions, and to the following: Bord Fáilte (Irish Tourist Board) 9, 97, 149; John Coleman, Esq. 98, 104; The Green Studio 6; National Library of Ireland, Dublin 3, 4, 16, 22, 38, 43, 66–68, 70, 88, 89, 108–110, 152; John O'Reilly, Esq. 81, 124; Edwin Smith 50; Eileen Tweedy 26, 83–85, 131, 138; Jane Williams Antiques 65.

INDEX

Page numbers in *italics* indicate illustrations